You Can Rest

100 DEVOTIONS TO CALM YOUR HEART AND MIND

BY KATY BOATMAN

B&H
PUBLISHING GROUP
Nashville, Tennessee

For my nieces, Shelby and Ellie.
May you always know that Jesus is with you,
and because of who He is, you can rest.

Published by B&H Publishing Group,
Nashville, Tennessee

Dewey Decimal Classification: J242.62
Subject Heading: DEVOTIONAL LITERATURE / GIRLS / ANXIETY

1 2 3 4 5 6 7 • 25 24 23 22 21

Contents

Introduction

I know you have plenty of things to worry about.

How many times have you laid down in your bed at night only to have your mind take over your plans to fall asleep? Your brain tries to make you remember all the things that went wrong that day, the things you are nervous about for tomorrow, and everything you're scared of as it gets dark! Before you know it, you are wide awake—worrying that you will be awake all night—and the worry wheel is spinning out of control.

God knows and understands this worry. He's there to help you fight it. God sees and hears all those worries that are distracting you at school, making you anxious, and keeping you awake at night.

This book contains one hundred different devotions to read before bed (or anytime!). They'll help you realize what God can do with your worry, remind you that He's with you, and help you go to sleep thinking about how much He loves you.

After every ten days of devotions, there is a question for you to answer and some lines where you can journal. Consider those pages your chance to write out your honest thoughts and feelings. You can answer the question given and continue to write out what is on your heart. These pages are for you! Don't worry about making everything sound nice—just write out what you're thinking. This is your safe space to process, reflect, and be still. You can even write your prayers to God if that's helpful to you. He wants to hear what is on your mind.

There's also a full index in the back of the book where you can look up different things you might be worrying about and see if there is a devotion on that topic. If you climb in bed one night and you're worried about school, or your family, or making friends, you can head to the index, look up those topics, and find out which pages to turn to for help. My prayer is that whether you go through the book from Day 1 to 100 or skip around to find the topics that relate to you the most, you'll encounter the God who will never leave you—the God who cares about your feelings.

I wrote this devotional not because I no longer struggle with worry, but because I know now what to do with my worry when it comes. I run to God. My prayer is that you would walk away from reading this with a sense of peace—because you, too, know that God is with you.

God is not scared.

God can help you.

God will take care of tomorrow.

God can give you peace.

And God is with you.

Rest in that. Rest in Him.

A Note About Asking for Professional Help

As we talk about things that worry us, I want you to know it's okay to seek professional help! Some worries and problems are too big to handle alone. Some of the topics we're going to talk about in this book may be an overwhelming issue for you and something that reading a short devotion can't help solve. If you're battling those things or dealing with a diagnosis of anxiety or depression, it is absolutely okay (and necessary) to reach out to doctors, counselors, pastors, teachers, and parents for extra help and support. No one is supposed to carry these anxieties alone. You are so loved.

You Can Rest

God proves his own love for us in that while we were still sinners, Christ died for us.—ROMANS 5:8

There are so many things that worry our minds, and we'll talk about a lot of those throughout this book. There's one thing, however, that I want to make sure you know before anything else.

Jesus died for you, so you can rest.

Let me tell you more about what that means. We are all born broken people. You, me, your parents, your friends. So if you're worried that you've messed up too much or you don't feel like you're enough, the truth is—none of us is enough.

God created people to be with Him, but because of our sinful and broken nature, we are separated from God. There is nothing we can do on our own to fix that. Trying to be nice enough, read the Bible enough, or be respectful enough won't fill the separation gap between us and God. Plus, all the trying so hard is just exhausting.

But here's where the good news comes in: God sent His Son, Jesus, to live on earth and to die in our place so we can be forgiven for all our mistakes. When we trust in Jesus and begin a relationship with Him, we get to spend forever with God. And that starts immediately.

This is why you can rest. When you have a relationship with Jesus, you are forgiven. You don't have to worry about not being enough, because Jesus is. You don't have to stress over being perfect at everything, because Jesus is. And you don't have to live without God, ever, because He lives in you.

Rest in that.

God, I know I need You in my life. I want to know You more and trust You. Will You come into my life and come into my heart? Thank You for giving me the chance to be with You forever.

DAY 2

When You're Scared

"When you pass through the waters, I will be with you, and the rivers will not overwhelm you. When you walk through the fire, you will not be scorched, and the flame will not burn you."—ISAIAH 43:2

Did anything make you scared today?

There is something about nighttime that can bring up all our fears, no matter how old we are. But God tells us over and over again in the Bible to not fear. It's a reminder that He is in control and we are not—and this is such a relief!

If you read chapter 43 of Isaiah, you see just how many things God was prepared to rescue His people from. And that's still true today.

You may not be passing through water or fire, but you no doubt have lots of scary things going on around you because this world is broken!

Now, you may read this verse and think that God's people never get hurt or that He always makes life easy. But we have to remember to look at the Bible as a whole and not just at one verse. There are plenty of times in Scripture when God's people were hurt or suffering (like in the book of Job). The people in the Bible were scared a lot too, and God did not promise to take the scary things away. Instead, He promised us *Himself.* That's the gift!

When we are scared, He is our safe place (Psalm 46:1). He is our shelter from the storm (Isaiah 4:6). We can trust in Him (Psalm 145:19).

God is our refuge & strength an ever-present help in trouble

↳ It will be a shelter and shade from the heat of the day and a refuge and hiding place from the storm and rain

He fulfills the desires of those who fear him he hears their cry and saves them

Whatever you named at the start of today's reading does not have to be the last thing on your mind as you fall asleep. God has called you by name. He is whispering, "Hey, I know you're scared, and that's okay because You are mine. I've got this."

Rest in that.

God, would You take away my fear? Will You remind me that You are in control? Thank You for being my safe place.

Isaiah 43:1 But now thus says the lord, he who created you, O Jacob, he who formed you O Israel "Fear not, for I have redeemed you; I have called you by name, you are mine.

When You Want to Do It All Yourself

Therefore, we may boldly say, "The Lord is my helper; I will not be afraid. What can man do to me?"—HEBREWS 13:6

Have you ever watched a baby learn to walk? Those wobbly legs fight to keep their balance, yet gravity wins, and the baby plops right back down to the floor! So, what do they do next?

When they can't quite get the momentum they need, babies know how to get moving faster. Finding the closest piece of furniture to grab onto or a hand to hold, they pull themselves up and start going on their merry way, with the help of something to steady them. Babies are smart!

As humans, sometimes our desire to do everything on our own means we fall down a lot. As we get older, we want to prove that we can do a lot more than walk—we can handle all the homework without taking notes, we can remember the words to the play without practicing much, and we can navigate friendships without involving adults.

And you know what? Sometimes you can do all of that. But it won't take long until you can't fall asleep because you're trying to remember your lines; you're stressing about grades; you're anxious about the drama. Bottom line, you become overwhelmed.

But guess what? You have help! Not only can God help you, but He provides other people to be a steady hand to hold.

Being independent and "walking on your own" means also making smart choices—and that includes using help when you have access to it. You will be able to handle the worry when you use the resources around you. Rehearse your lines with a friend. Take notes in class and make to-do lists. Ask a teacher, parent, or mentor for wisdom when you're having trouble with friends.

And ask God for strength. He is strong, which means you can lean on Him to help you through it all.

Rest in that.

I want to do things on my own, but I know I can't do everything! God, thank You for helping me. Thank You for friends and family who love me and help me too.

When You're Afraid of the Dark

Even the darkness is not dark to you. The night shines like the day; darkness and light are alike to you.—PSALM 139:12

Have you ever played hide-and-seek in the dark? As you crouch down in your spot, the suspense of waiting for someone to find you is so scary! In the pitch-black darkness, you listen closely for the person searching for you, and sometimes all you can hear is the sound of your own breath.

I don't like the dark in general, so I hate playing games in the dark. If I were hiding, I'd choose a room near a window so some light could still get in. When I am trying to sleep at night, I leave a small light on so I can still distinguish everything in my room. I don't like the dark because I can't see in it.

Our minds sometimes come up with crazy ideas in the darkness. Whatever we can't see, we imagine to be something scary. When we can't see, we often react to what we think is there. What if we could shine some light in the darkness?

Whether you're playing hide-and-seek in the dark, it's time to fall asleep, or the darkness is something you're feeling inside, let me tell you the truth about darkness: God can see in the dark, and He is not afraid of it.

The Bible tells us that darkness is just as light as daytime to Him. That means God knows where you should step when walking in the dark, *and* He knows what's coming your way in the future, which you can't see.

Whatever kind of darkness is scaring you, ask God to shine some light on it. Ask God to make it brighter. And remember that even if you still can't see in the dark, He can.

Rest in that.

God, thank You for being my light in the darkness. Help me trust You with what I cannot see.

When It Storms

He got up, rebuked the wind, and said to the sea, "Silence! Be still!" The wind ceased, and there was a great calm. Then he said to them, "Why are you afraid? Do you still have no faith?" And they were terrified and asked one another, "Who then is this? Even the wind and the sea obey him!"—MARK 4:39–41

There's something magical (but also nerve-wracking!) about a storm, when the lightning and thunder team up to light up the sky and sound off at the same time. It is so startling!

Storms are loud, and they can be scary. It's okay if they make you nervous!

Have you ever wondered what Jesus thought of storms? Mark 4 gives us a glimpse of Jesus' interaction with a storm. He was out in a boat with the disciples, who were acting like we'd expect people caught in a storm to act: they were freaking out! Jesus, on the other hand, was fast asleep.

The disciples woke Jesus up, asking if He didn't care if they all died in the storm. Jesus then commanded the sea and storm to be still. Both came to a stop.

How was Jesus able to sleep during a storm that was so crazy the disciples thought they would die? He had such peace because He is the Son of God. This Jesus, the One who sleeps through storms, is with us when the storms of life are happening around us.

Life's storms might be a fight you're in with your friends. It might be dealing with your parents' disapproval or divorce.

Now, I won't tell you that Jesus will calm every storm you are in, because I can't predict that. But I will tell you that He will sit with you in it. Comfort is found not just when the storm goes away. Comfort in the middle of a storm is being with Jesus Himself. He is capable of settling it, but He's also capable of calming your mind and heart. He will not leave you. He will not let you go. His peaceful presence changes everything.

Rest in that.

God, I don't like storms (of any kind), and this is really hard. Will You calm my heart and mind through them? Thank You for being right here with me. I know I am safe in Your arms.

DAY 6

When You're Worried About Tomorrow

"Don't worry about tomorrow, because tomorrow will worry about itself. Each day has enough trouble of its own."—MATTHEW 6:34

Have you heard of the Sunday Scaries? It's the term we use to describe our feelings when the weekend is coming to an end and the responsibilities of Monday are on our minds. The truth is, sometimes we get the Monday Scaries, the Tuesday Scaries, or the No-Matter-What-Day-It-Is Scaries. I know this is true for me!

In the book of Matthew, Jesus reminds us not to be anxious. He says, "Consider the birds of the sky: They don't sow or reap or gather into barns, yet your heavenly Father feeds them. Aren't you worth more than they?" (Matthew 6:26).

Jesus talks about the flowers too. They aren't spinning out of control in worry as they bloom and grow. They aren't worried about tomorrow because God provides for the birds and the flowers every single day. And He'll provide for you too.

Our worry can often translate into a need to control what happens tomorrow. We worry about our family's health, our to-do list, or if our friends will still like us. But can you imagine the birds doing that? Do you think they fly around worried they won't find a tree branch to rest on? Do you think they fall asleep wondering if they will find worms to feed their babies in the morning? God created the birds and everything they need—and He created you too. Do you think God's worried about what will happen tomorrow?

As you fall asleep tonight, think about God's creation. The trees aren't worried about blossoming tomorrow. The grass isn't worried about growing tomorrow. The sun isn't worried about rising tomorrow. God's creation continues to work to the sound of His voice, and He will care for you both today *and* tomorrow.

Rest in that.

God, thank You for reminding me You're in control when I'm worried about what might happen tomorrow. Thank You for making the sun rise and the world spin every day. Will You continue to remind me that tomorrow is in Your hands?

When You Hate Not Knowing What's Coming

In the hope of eternal life that God, who cannot lie, promised before time began.—TITUS 1:2

Do you like roller coasters? I think they're so fun! Well, some of them.

When I'm standing in line, I always try to watch the people who are already on the ride. I want to see how many times they go upside down and how big the drop is (and hear how loud they scream!). I like to know what to expect.

This is actually true of me all of the time: I want to know what's coming.

Every Sunday night, I look at my calendar to see what the next week's schedule is. Do I have a lot of meetings? Do I have anything fun planned? Do I have a lot of free time? It helps me prepare my mind for what's to come.

As you lie in bed at night, are you like me? Do you think about all the things ahead? Sometimes I can get so caught up in this that I become afraid when *I don't know* what's coming. It's just like the roller coaster! I want to see all the twists and turns it takes before I get on, but sometimes there are crazy turns you just can't see from standing in line.

When I start to fear, I remind myself that God is all-knowing. This means that what happened yesterday, what happens today, and what will happen tomorrow, He already knows. This means I can put my mind to rest because even if I don't know what's coming, He does. Also, I trust Him. He's never failed me.

And think about this: Because the Bible tells us the whole story of God's creation, we already know how things will end. There will be a day when Jesus returns to earth to restore it, and we'll spend forever with God. So we don't know what the future holds, but we do know we will spend it with God, the One who is all-knowing! And that's our hope—forever with Him.

Rest in that.

God, it helps me so much to remember You know everything that's coming, and that no matter what, I get to be with You. Will You help me trust in Your plan? Thank You, God. I love You.

When You're Too Excited to Sleep

This is the day the LORD has made; let's rejoice and be glad in it.—PSALM 118:24

I remember the time I had to keep a big secret: my brother and sister-in-law were going to surprise my niece and nephew with a puppy.

When I was brought in on the plan, I may have been more excited than anyone. It was my job to watch a movie with the kids while their parents picked up the puppy. So the night before, all I could think about was the secret schedule for the next day, and how excited the kids would be once the puppy arrived. I tossed and turned all night!

Whether it's the night before Christmas, our birthday, or the first day of school, excitement and expectation can take control of our minds . . . so much that we can't sleep a wink!

When this happens, remind yourself to *be present*. That means to focus on what's going on right at the moment. If you're lying in bed, focus on the softness of your blankets and pillow. Take deep breaths. Listen to the quiet. Bring your mind back to falling asleep instead of letting it run away with future plans. When we get so excited about what's coming that we don't sleep at all, we find ourselves exhausted on the day we've been waiting on for so long! When this happens, here's what I suggest.

Focus on today: What are you grateful for in this very moment?

Focus on giving thanks: What can you thank God for now?

Ask God to calm your mind, and not take away your joy: What can you celebrate about today as you go to sleep?

Remember, God can give you rest in the middle of your excitement.

Rest in that.

I am so excited, God! Will You help me stay present in the moment so I don't miss what You're doing right now? Thank You for what You've done for me, and what You're going to do!

DAY 9

When It's Hard to Be Still

"Do not fear, for I am with you; do not be afraid, for I am your God. I will strengthen you; I will help you; I will hold on to you with my righteous right hand."—ISAIAH 41:10

Do you ever lie in your bed and wonder what that strange noise was outside your window? Or you remember something scary, and you can't get it off your mind? All of a sudden, those noises and thoughts make you wish you weren't alone. You long to run out of your room and find a family member to remind you that everything is okay.

What if you started to pray in those moments? What if you told God you were feeling alone and asked Him to remind you that He's right there? He is eager for you to be still in His presence (Psalm 46:10).

It can sometimes be hard to remember that God is always with us because we can't physically see Him. But think about the wind. You can feel it blowing against your skin and watch it taking the leaves off the trees. Even though you can't physically see it, the wind's presence is obvious, and so is God's.

We can feel God's love, see His creation, and read His words in the Bible. Plus, we have the Holy Spirit living inside us as our Helper. It's okay to *feel* alone, but we are never truly alone. Knowing this helps us to be still.

So when your mind is distracted by outside noises or thoughts spiraling in your head, ask God to help. Being still is not a punishment. It's a moment to pause, take a deep breath, and rest. It's a moment to accept God's offer of peace and calm.

Rest in that.

God, thank You for always being with me. I want to be able to be still in Your presence. If I get scared tonight, would You remind me that You're right here?

When You Have a Nightmare

"The LORD will fight for you, and you must be quiet."
—EXODUS 14:14

Let's talk about nightmares. They are the worst, right? So, what do we do about them?

If you wake up after having one, and your heart is still racing as you try to figure out what's real and what's not, the first thing to do is start praying. Ask God to calm your mind and heart. Ask Him to take away the memory of the nightmare, then tell the devil that he has no place in your mind. Sometimes the enemy wants to take over your mind, but God is in control there. In the name of Jesus, command the devil to stay out of your thoughts.

God can fight the nightmares. Let Him.

If you're too worried to fall asleep because you're scared you're going to have a nightmare, Matthew 19 might bring you some peace. It's one of my favorite examples of Jesus' gentleness in the Bible. Jesus was in Jordan, where a lot of people were looking for Him and bombarding Him with questions. Then in Matthew 19:13–14, people started bringing their children to Him.

The disciples tried to prevent the children from getting to Jesus, but He shut it down. Jesus not only invited the children over, He reminded everyone present that the kingdom of God belongs to children too!

Tonight, as you begin to fall asleep, set your mind on this scene. Jesus invites you to come to Him. The kingdom of God belongs to you too. No matter who or what distracts you, scares you, or tries to stand in your way, Jesus wants to be with you. Your dreams and your life are safe with Him. God will fight for you.

Rest in that.

God, will You protect my dreams tonight? Will You give me a night of peaceful rest? You are a good God.

JOURNALING PAGES

What have you been worried about lately? Write those things out like a letter to God. Let Him know what's on your mind.

What have you learned about God so far that has been comforting to you?

_____

_____

_____

_____

_____

_____

_____

_____

_____

_____

_____

_____

_____

DAY 11

When You're Waiting for an Answer

Now the mindset of the flesh is death, but the mindset of the Spirit is life and peace.—ROMANS 8:6

When I was ten, I auditioned for a choir that performed at different events and gatherings around town. While I was excited about the idea, my stomach was also doing flips. It's scary to try out for something, right? I remember thinking, *What if I mess up? What if I forget the words? What if I don't know the answer to the director's question?*

What I didn't realize, though, is that the audition itself wouldn't be the only hard part. Waiting to find out if I got a spot in the choir also sent my stomach jumping around like it was on a trampoline.

When we're excited about the possibility of something that may or may not happen, we can get worked up in the waiting.

Will I make the team?

Will I get the part?

Will they let me play?

Do we have to move?

Will I get what I want?

There's something we can learn while we wait that will help us in every situation: whether the answer is *yes, no,* or *maybe,* God's plan is always better than our own.

It's okay to be sad if we don't get what we want, but God is teaching us something while we wait, and He's teaching us something with the way He answers. His plans for you are good, whether you can see it right now or not. And when you ask Him for something, remember that no matter what His answer, He always offers love, joy, peace, patience, kindness, goodness, gentleness, and self-control in the midst of it (Galatians 5:22–23). God always has something good for us in the waiting because that is who He is.

Rest in that.

God, would You remind me when I'm waiting that You have a good plan in mind no matter what happens? Would You give me peace tonight while I wait?

When You Think No One Takes You Seriously

Then David said, "The LORD who rescued me from the paw of the lion and the paw of the bear will rescue me from the hand of this Philistine."—1 SAMUEL 17:37

Have you heard the story of David and Goliath? David was a young shepherd, which meant his job was to watch over the sheep—and sheep aren't very clever. They need to be watched over.

One day a Philistine man named Goliath showed up to battle the Israelites, and he was nine feet, nine inches tall. A giant! His size was so intimidating that no one wanted to fight him.

David was young and small, and no one took him seriously, but God doesn't care how young we are. He can work through anyone. David took one rock and a slingshot and was able to defeat Goliath! The young, small shepherd boy, whom everyone doubted, won the battle.

Do you ever feel like people don't take you seriously?

I am part of the greeting team at my church where we say hello to people as they walk in on a Sunday. When the other greeters and I gather before the church service to pray, my favorite part is when a kid volunteers to lead us in prayer. They greet alongside their parents, but their faith and joy light up the room. It makes my day every time I see them.

You are not too young for God to work through.

In fact, your faith in God speaks volumes to us adults, who so often forget what it's like to just let go and trust God. You're more concerned about loving God than figuring out all the ins and outs about Him, and that is something many adults can learn from.

As someone who is young, you are important to the work of God on this earth.

Rest in that.

Thank You for reminding me that I matter, God! When I feel like people don't see me, would You show me they do, and would You work through me?

When Everything Is Spinning

They will be called righteous trees, planted by the LORD to glorify him.—ISAIAH 61:3

I get car sick easily. When it's hard to see out of the windows or the road gets windy, my stomach and my head do not play well together, and soon things start spinning. Do you ever feel this way about everything going on around you?

Maybe you and your parents are trying to make a decision about what school to go to next year. Maybe you're waiting to find out about your dad's job and if your family has to move. Maybe you are dying to hear if your best friend is going to be in your class next school year. Whatever the case, sometimes it feels like everything is changing around us, yet we are left standing in the middle, while it spins out of control.

In another translation of the Bible (NIV), today's verse refers to God's people as "oaks of righteousness." Do you know why I like that phrase? An oak is a tree that's tall and firm and steady. Its branches may sway in the wind, but it stands upright.

We know even the strongest trees can fall, though. A bad storm may knock one down, or someone may come along and cut it down. But if we are planted by the Lord, our tree roots are in *Him*. The unshakable and steady One. The One who can't be torn down.

So when you feel like a tree being blown around in the wind, when you feel like your life is spinning out of control, when you feel like you're too dizzy to even see straight, remember where your roots are: in the unmoving, unfailing love of God. He is not surprised by the changes, and He will continue to hold you steady with every move ahead.

Rest in that.

God, thank You for helping me stay steady when things feel crazy. Remind me that my roots are in You, so I am secure.

When You're Not a Good Enough Friend

Be kind and compassionate to one another, forgiving one another, just as God also forgave you in Christ.
—EPHESIANS 4:32

Friends are a gift. They make us laugh, they listen to our stories, and they help us when we need it. How special it is to have someone you can count on (and someone who will laugh at your jokes even if they're bad)!

Do you ever worry if you're being a good enough friend?

Being a good friend can be challenging. You might stress out about doing whatever your friend wants to do or making sure they don't ditch you for a cooler friend. Plus, neither one of you is a perfect person, which means at one point or another, you will hurt each other's feelings. Then there's the difficulty of making new friends. Maybe one of you doesn't feel comfortable being yourself, or you struggle to find something in common. All this is normal.

So, how do you know how to be a good friend?

Jesus tells us in the book of Mark to love our neighbors like we would love ourselves (Mark 12:31). Or maybe you've heard of the Golden Rule: "Treat others like you would want to be treated." This comes from Matthew 7:12.

We all want to hang out with someone who is kind, compassionate, and forgives us when we're wrong. This is a good friend! So when you're not sure if you're being a good friend, remember to live that way. You don't have to worry if you're cool enough to be the kind of friend people want. If you're kind and compassionate with others, that's the kind of friend people need.

And you know what? When you show your friends kindness and love them even when it's hard, you show them a glimpse of what Jesus is like. And that's the best way to be a good friend.

Rest in that.

God, thank You for my friends. Will You help me be kind and love them well? Will You remind me that treating people the way Jesus treated people is more important than trying to be cool?

DAY 15

When You Want to Hide

"Can a person hide in secret places where I cannot see him?"
—the LORD's declaration. "Do I not fill the heavens and the
earth?"—the LORD's declaration.—JEREMIAH 23:24

As I was sitting on the beach recently, I watched a tiny crab
pop up out from the sand. He crawled around, checked out
what was happening, and quickly scurried back inside his
little hole when he realized I was near his space. I watched
him slowly try again—come back out, glance around, and
immediately dart back to his hole as soon he was scared. He
did this over and over.

This crab had me imagining what it would be like to hide in
a hole whenever I wanted to. How many times would I run
back when I was scared? How often would I head into my
dark corner when I knew I'd messed up and didn't want anyone to find me?

We may not have holes in the sand, but we do hide a lot, don't
we? Sometimes we hide what we're feeling because we don't
want to talk about it. Sometimes we hide what we've done

because we know it was wrong. And sometimes we hide who we are because we think no one will like us.

But here's the thing: you cannot hide from God. While that may seem intimidating, it's a wonderful invitation to come to God with whatever—yes, *whatever*—you're feeling. He already knows!

There's nothing you will do (or have already done) that will change the way God feels about you. When He looks at you, He's delighted. When He thinks about you, He smiles. His love for you is bigger than any mistake you've made and stronger than your deepest fear.

Inside the holes we try to hide in, God is waiting to remind you that you are seen and loved at the very same time.

Rest in that.

God, sometimes I don't want to admit when I'm wrong or talk about what's making me sad and scared. But thank You for always loving me anyway. No matter what!

When You're Not Sure If God Loves You

God saw all that he had made, and it was very good indeed.
—GENESIS 1:31

W hen you brushed your teeth before bed tonight, you probably looked at yourself in the mirror. What did you think when you saw yourself? Were you concerned about getting the cookie you had for dessert out of your teeth? Were you wondering if your hair was sticking out like that all day? Were you already thinking about everything you had to do tomorrow?

It's amazing the number of thoughts that fly through our minds during a simple task like brushing our teeth!

What if every time you looked at yourself in the mirror you remembered to thank God for His love for you? So many of the worries that float around in our brains do so because we forget that the God who created the entire world created us too. And the Bible tells us that what God created, He called "good." As you stare at the mirror, let that reminder be the thing your mind turns to instead of all of the worries from the day.

God loves what He made, and He especially loves you! Despite the fact that today may have been hard or overwhelming or frustrating, God did not change His mind about you. He is not going anywhere; in fact, He has had a loving plan for your life even before you were born.

So tonight, as you lay your head on your pillow, thank God for His love. It is not based on what you did today or what you will do tomorrow. His love is here to stay.

Rest in that.

God, thank You for loving me no matter what. Will You help my mind focus on Your love as I fall asleep, and remind me that I can always tell You how I'm feeling? I love You, God.

DAY 17

When You're So Tired You Could Cry

Because of the LORD's faithful love we do not perish, for his mercies never end. They are new every morning; great is your faithfulness!—LAMENTATIONS 3:22–23

Do you know those days when both your brain and body are super tired? Sometimes you don't even realize it. You are teary or angry or in a terrible mood, and later you realize it's because you are past the state of tired—you're *utterly exhausted*.

I have those days too.

Recently, I didn't feel well for an entire week, and I had so much work to do. At the end of each day, my mind was so full that words were hard to say, and my body was so tired that it was hard to move. All I wanted to do was fall into my bed and go to sleep.

And that's okay! We all have days like this—days when we cry, days when we are too tired to function, and days when we are too worried to focus. When that happens to you, it doesn't mean anything is wrong with you. It simply means you are a human and had a hard day.

When those days come, here's what I want you to do: Think about what you are thankful for. When you're crying and don't know why, or when you are too tired to function, ask yourself, *What was good about today? Who am I grateful for today? What has God done for me?*

When things are hard and we think about what is good, we are thankful that not every day is hard.

When things are stressful and we think about what we love, we are thankful that we are not alone.

When we have no strength and we think about God, we are thankful that He can help us keep going.

Then, after being thankful, get some rest! Tomorrow is a fresh start.

Rest in that.

God, thank You for family and thank You for friends. Thank You for always being there for me even on the hard days. Would You give me rest tonight?

When You Have to Be Patient

A patient person shows great understanding, but a quick-tempered one promotes foolishness.—PROVERBS 14:29

Patience. It's not a word I much care for. Do you? When someone's telling me to be patient, or I know I'm in a situation when I need patience, it means there's something I desperately want but don't have yet (like waiting for a fun vacation to start). Rather than wait, I want it *now*. Can you relate?

You don't want to wait for dinner to be ready. You don't want to wait to find out if you got the part in the school play. You don't want to wait for your dad to get home from his work trip. You don't want to wait until your friend returns from summer camp. You're ready to eat. To perform. To see your dad. To play with your friend. You're ready. Why isn't the rest of the world?

The Bible talks a lot about patience. Patience is a choice; it's something we adjust in our attitudes. It is uncomfortable, but it helps us grow. With the Holy Spirit, we are capable of choosing patience, even when we don't automatically feel it.

Abraham and Sarah were a married couple in the Bible who experienced the longing to have a baby. In Genesis 17, God promised He would give them a child, and in Genesis 21, their son, Isaac, was born. But Abraham and Sarah were both really old at that point; Abraham was around a hundred and Sarah around ninety. Can you imagine the patience it took to wait on God's timing?

God always has a plan. When we have a hard time waiting, we can ask Jesus to give us both the patience to wait on God's timing and the strength to wait calmly. He lives in us, remember? He's strong enough to carry the burden of waiting for us.

Rest in that.

Jesus, I'm not very good at waiting! Will You help me be patient and trust that Your plan for me is better than what I have in mind?

When You Don't Know How to Pray

This is the confidence we have before him: if we ask anything according to his will, he hears us.—1 JOHN 5:14

I think one of the most hilarious games is Telephone. Do you know it? One person whispers something into another person's ear, and that person then whispers it to the next person. It goes on and on down the line until the last person shouts out what was said. It never fails that by the time the message gets to the final person, it's radically different from the original.

Original message: Ellie got a kitten. *What the last person says:* Smelly bought a mitten?!?

While this game is fun, sometimes we might think we're playing a game of Telephone with God too, which isn't as fun. We worry about praying correctly. *God, did You hear what I said? Did that make sense? Are You sure You heard everything right?*

It's easy to think there's a formula to praying—that we have to speak in a formal way or say things in a particular order. The truth is God just wants you to talk to Him. He is your

Creator and our Father, so He deserves honor and respect as you approach Him, *and* He wants you to tell Him everything as you would your closest friend.

When we're worried too much about praying correctly, it leads us to not pray at all. So don't overthink it. Spend time with God. Talk to Him. Listen for Him. Trust that He has heard you correctly. The more you do, the closer you'll grow to Him and the more confident you'll be in your prayers.

God knows your voice because He made you. He knows your heart because He lives in it. And He knows what you're saying because He's not a God of confusion (1 Corinthians 14:33). If nothing seems clear to you, remember that everything is clear to Him. Let Him lead the way.

Rest in that.

Hey, God. I just want to talk to You like a friend. I know You hear me and love me. Thank You for reminding me that You understand me.

DAY 20

When You Feel Left Out

"What do you think? If someone has a hundred sheep, and one of them goes astray, won't he leave the ninety-nine on the hillside and go and search for the stray?"—MATTHEW 18:12

Have you ever found out that your friends were all hanging out without you? Or maybe you learned there was a birthday party coming up that you weren't invited to.

The feeling of being left out stings. It can make you feel anxious and lonely. You start trying to figure out what you could have done or said differently so you would be included. You might even make a long list in your mind of all the things that are wrong with you.

Being left out of fun plans doesn't mean you are not loved. It simply means sometimes humans forget about other humans. It means sometimes people are selfish and don't think about other people's feelings. It means sometimes friends will let you down.

Whenever I feel lonely or left out, I try to remember an important truth about God: He is a Shepherd. Now, this may feel like a strange thing to think about because we don't see shepherds often anymore. But a shepherd's job is to be attentive to his sheep. In Matthew 18:12 Jesus tells a story about a shepherd who has one hundred sheep, but one of them gets away. The man doesn't hesitate to leave the ninety-nine other sheep to go find the one that went missing! In the same way, God will come find you. You are never alone or forgotten.

If you have recently been left out, if it seems like no one wants to hang out with you, or if you feel like no one sees you, remember God will come looking for you. He attends to His sheep. You're not invisible to Him.

Rest in that.

Thank You, God, for always being with me and reminding me that You will not leave me out or forget about me. Will You reassure me that You always see me? Thank You for being my Shepherd.

JOURNALING PAGES

Write about some of the things that have made you cry lately and why. Do you feel comfortable letting others see you cry and sharing what's wrong? Who is a safe person you could talk to about what's been troubling you?

What helps calm your heart and mind when you're worried, sad, or scared? Try to think of as many things as possible, and try to be as honest as possible. (Not everything that calms us may be something we are proud of, and that's okay. When we're honest, we can let God help us.)

When You Can't Wait to Have Fun

Rejoice in hope; be patient in affliction; be persistent in prayer.—ROMANS 12:12

Sometimes we live in a series of "can't waits." You can't wait until summer camp is here. You can't wait until it's Christmas. You can't wait until you're old enough to have a cell phone. You can't wait until school is out. You can't wait to drive.

Whatever the thing may be, the anticipation for it can feel more emotional than the actual moment you are waiting on! It's fun to be excited about something that's still to come, but what does this "can't wait" feeling do to your heart? Have your positive feelings ever given way to negative ones? For example, do you become anxious? Annoyed or frustrated? How about impatient?

As you wait for exciting things, "rejoice in hope" as Romans 12:12 reminds us. Remember that every good gift comes from "the Father of lights" (James 1:17) and that God's timing is better than ours. Be content in your current circumstances too. Take any impatience to Jesus in prayer.

Do you know what I can't wait for? I can't wait for the day Jesus returns! The day He restores the earth to what it once was and we live in peace forever with Him. This will be the most exciting thing ever! But the days of waiting for it are long. Sometimes I let the positive feeling of waiting for Jesus give way to my negative thoughts. Sometimes I get too focused on myself and forget to rejoice in hope and choose joy.

The day will come when we no longer have to wait for good things, and all we will know is joy. But guess what? Jesus isn't hiding from you until that day. He's with you, even now, as you wait.

Rest in that.

God, there are so many things I'm waiting for! Would You help me be patient and hopeful while I wait?

DAY 22

When You Need to Be Honest

Do not lie to one another, since you have put off the old self with its practices and have put on the new self. You are being renewed in knowledge according to the image of your Creator.—COLOSSIANS 3:9–10

When I was five, I stood at the door of my parents' bedroom as my mom asked me if I had cut my own hair. With scissors in my hand, and strands of hair that clearly didn't line up with the rest, I said what I thought might keep me out of trouble: "No."

There was no denying this was a lie.

We can find ourselves tempted to lie for so many reasons. Sometimes we don't want to get in trouble. (Cutting my own hair definitely wasn't an approved activity!) Sometimes we think the truth will hurt someone or will make things more complicated. These mind games we play—trying to decide whether to tell the truth or hide it—weigh heavily on us, and we spend too much time stressing out over it.

Being honest is a better way to live.

Yes, being honest may lead to an uncomfortable conversation. It may mean getting into trouble. It may end up upsetting someone else. But following Jesus means living the way He did, and Jesus was honest. Honesty always brings truth into the light, so we can see what's really there (Ephesians 5:13).

When you follow Jesus, you don't have to worry or control other people through lies. But if you do give into temptation and lie, confess that to Jesus and ask forgiveness from others. Then trust God with the consequences. He's not scared of your truth or your lie.

Rest in that.

God, thank You for always forgiving me when I come to You. Thank You for giving me courage when I'm scared to tell the truth. Help me to be honest with my friends and my family even when it's hard.

DAY 23

When You Wish Things Had Gone Differently

Confess your sins to one another and pray for one another, so that you may be healed. The prayer of a righteous person is very powerful in its effect.—James 5:16

When I was in the second grade, a teacher pulled me and a friend into the hallway to ask about an incident that happened on the playground. I knew we were in trouble. As a kid who always wanted to be liked by the teacher, I not only was upset over being pulled into the hallway, but I regretted what we had done—made fun of another student.

I can feel the redness of my cheeks and the churning in my stomach when I think back on that day—and all the other times I've hurt someone's feelings. The times I've said something I should not have. The times I spewed angry words. The times I've remained silent when I should have spoken up. It still makes me sad to think about.

Do those moments stick in your mind too?

One thing I wish I had known more about when I was younger was *forgiveness*. We will all hurt each other's feelings because we're all messed-up people (it's why Jesus came to save us!). But when you've hurt someone, instead of thinking about what you've done over and over, what can you do?

As today's Bible verse says, you can go to the person and tell them you're sorry. Ask them to forgive you. Pray for them, and ask God to forgive you as well. I know this is hard and scary, but it will be worth it to strengthen your relationship with that person and with God.

And you know what? God will forgive! Just as an eraser wipes away the words on a white board, God will wipe away your mistakes, and you get to start over (1 John 1:7).

This wiping away is called forgiveness, and because of it, you can rest.

Rest in that.

God, would You show me if I've hurt someone's feelings? Would You help me ask for forgiveness? Thank You for Your forgiveness.

DAY 24

When You're Trying to Get Everything Right

My dear brothers and sisters, be steadfast, immovable, always excelling in the Lord's work, because you know that your labor in the Lord is not in vain.—1 CORINTHIANS 15:58

Did you ever play the game Pin the Tail on the Donkey? In the game, someone puts on a blindfold and takes a pretend tail in their hand. Then someone else spins the blindfolded person around for a few seconds. Confused and a little dizzy, the blindfolded person tries to place the tail in the right spot on the donkey poster.

Sometimes the person makes it to the poster but pins the tail in a silly spot—like on the donkey's head! Sometimes, they're not even close and pin the tail on the wall far away from the poster. It's such a funny sight to watch.

Do you ever feel like life is a little like Pin the Tail on the Donkey? You know people's expectations, but it's not always easy to meet them. Sometimes it feels like you're blind and disoriented, and you find yourself asking, *Did I do okay?*

Life may feel like you're spinning—because of all the things being asked of you—but when that happens, focus on what matters. Keep doing your work. Keep being respectful and kind. Keep doing your best with what you have, and leave the rest up to God. Being obedient is far more important than the result. The Bible reminds us to be "steadfast" and "immovable" (1 Corinthians 15:58), and that often looks like just taking the next best step.

Finally, remember, the joy of a game like Pin the Tail on the Donkey is not just in putting the tail in the right spot. It's in the people standing around you who are watching, offering tips on which way to go, and cheering you on!

Your obedience and commitment are more important than your performance. Your willingness to try is more important than getting it perfect. And the people around you are there for a reason.

Rest in that.

Thank You, God, for all the people who love me and cheer me on! Would You help me be obedient and leave the rest up to You? Would You take the pressure away and help me rest in You?

When You Don't Know What to Wear

Put on the Lord Jesus Christ, and make no provision for the flesh to gratify its desires.—ROMANS 13:14

Clothes are so fun! As girls, we get to choose between jeans and dresses, leggings and shorts. We have shirts with flowers and shirts with stripes. Shoes that sparkle and shoes with heels. Hair bows, headbands, necklaces, bracelets, earrings, and so many more things to make outfits fun. It's a lot to choose from!

My number one reason for being late to school always had to do with my outfit. I wanted it to be just right. I wanted to feel cute and comfortable and in style all at the same time.

There's nothing wrong with liking clothes and fashion. But things can take a turn for the worse when our whole attitude changes because we can't find the perfect outfit, or we think our clothes aren't good enough compared to other girls.

When we start attaching our clothes to our emotions and our identities, things can turn upside down fast. Soon we've made clothes out to be a bigger issue than they should be. Our minds can take off with lies at that point too: *I'm not pretty enough. I don't have what other girls have. No one will like me.* None of this is good.

The next time this happens, instead of getting mad or frustrated about your outfit, try shifting your perspective and think about the things God tells us to put on: "Therefore, as God's chosen ones, holy and dearly loved, put on compassion, kindness, humility, gentleness, and patience" (Colossians 3:12).

The outfits you pick out every day will change, but what you choose to clothe your soul with will last. What if you were the girl who was known for her compassion, kindness, gentleness, and patience? Now *that's* something people would notice!

Rest in that.

God, thank You for fun clothes! Will You help me focus more on how I act and treat people than on what I wear? And on the days when I don't feel cute or cool, will You remind me that I'm precious and important to You?

DAY 26

When You Know It's Going to Hurt

The LORD will protect you from all harm; he will protect your life. The LORD will protect your coming and going both now and forever.—PSALM 121:7–8

No one likes getting a shot at the doctor's office. Even though the prick of a needle is typically quick, all we can think about before it happens is how much it's going to hurt. The last time I was at the doctor I didn't have to get a shot, but I had to get blood drawn and didn't know that until the last minute. This was probably for the best, because I didn't have long enough to start worrying about it!

Sometimes, like knowing you have to get a shot or blood drawn, you know something else painful is coming. Maybe your best friend is moving at the end of the school year, or you're going to have surgery soon. Maybe you're leaving one school to start over at a new one, or maybe one of your parents is moving out of your house. Whatever it may be, it can leave you dreading what's to come.

God knows it all, though. He knows what it will be like, and He will not leave you alone through any of it. When you think about how bad it's going to be, tell Him how you feel. When you're convinced it's too much to handle, God's love is big enough to carry you through it. And when the day you've been dreading arrives, look for God. He's right there with you in the hurt.

As you watch the nurse prepare your shot or your friend pack up to move, look for signs of God. He's in the nurse's smile, your friend's hug, and the deep breaths you take to stop the tears from flowing. It's okay to admit it hurts. Jesus is with you.

He's the best person to run to. Our protector. Our healer. Our safe place.

Rest in that.

God, thank You that I don't have to be alone when I'm hurting or sad. Thank You for always being my safe place.

When Friends Are Mean

"Blessed are the peacemakers, for they will be called sons of God."—MATTHEW 5:9

Do you ever find yourself replaying something mean someone said to you in your head? Sometimes that mean thing bothers us so much, it keeps us awake at night. You keep thinking back over it and going through all the emotions. First you're hurt. Then you're angry. Then you want to know why the person said what they said in the first place!

We are not responsible for our friends' actions or words, but we are responsible for the way we respond to them.

This can be tricky, especially when your feelings have been hurt. It's okay to tell your friend her words or actions hurt you. But it's important to remember you won't always know why someone acts the way they do. Maybe she's struggling deep down, but it's coming out as anger. Maybe she's under a lot of pressure or stressed out, so she's snappy and a little rude. None of these things are excuses, but they could be real reasons for someone's behavior.

Think about your own reactions to others. Have you ever been stressed or depressed, and you acted out in a way that might have hurt someone else? All of us do this from time to time. Because we receive grace from God, we can show grace to others.

So express how you feel with the hope of resolving it. Approach the situation as a peacemaker, offering kindness and care. And, most importantly, pray for your friend! If she continues to be mean, maybe you need to take a break from being friends with her and ask an adult for guidance. But you can always still pray for her (Matthew 5:44).

A friend's bad attitude is not a reflection of who you are. So instead of staying up all night worrying about her words, turn it around and pray instead. It'll change your heart, and it just might change hers too.

Rest in that.

God, thank You for friends. Will You help me be honest about my feelings when I'm hurt, and will You help me forgive those who hurt me?

When You're Sick

Be gracious to me, LORD, for I am weak; heal me, LORD, for my bones are shaking.—PSALM 6:2

Are you afraid of getting sick?

Whether it's a cold or COVID-19 or cancer, no one wants to get sick. There's so much unknown attached to all of it. Being sick means your body will suffer. It also means missing out on things. Maybe one day with no schoolwork and watching a movie isn't so bad. But when one day turns into one week, you start missing your friends, your routine, and having fun. You wonder, *How far behind with homework will I get? Is there a party I will miss? Will I have to go to the hospital?*

It's normal for your brain to do this, but because of Jesus, you have the power to pause and pray. After all, spending the time and energy on what-ifs will only make you more tired and more stressed out.

Plus, if you do wake up with a fever or find yourself at lots of doctor's offices, God will still be everything you need. Here are some truths to remember:

God is a healer (Jeremiah 30:17); He can take away the pain.

God is a sustainer (Psalm 54:4); He can carry you through all the symptoms when you feel like you don't have the strength.

God is your Father (Matthew 6:9); He will be right there with you when you don't feel well.

God is a provider (Philippians 4:19); He can bring the right doctors and medicines to you to help you heal.

Jesus came to heal the sick, not the healthy (Mark 2:17), and He can handle anything.

Rest in that.

Jesus, will You help me not worry about getting sick? Will You heal me when I don't feel well? Knowing that You can is the hope I need. Thank You for helping make sickness less scary.

When You Feel Too Much

I complain and groan morning, noon, and night, and he hears my voice.—PSALM 55:17

How are you feeling right now? We experience a wide variety of emotions in just one day. Maybe you woke up excited about seeing friends today, and then your brother did something to annoy you. All of a sudden you got frustrated and angry about everything. Maybe you woke up nervous about a test you had to take, but then your dad surprised you with chocolate chip pancakes! Right away, you were in a much better mood.

Our emotions can be all over the place: happy, sad, lonely, excited, scared, nervous, angry, joyful. Are you ever afraid to share your true emotions with the people around you because you are not sure of how they will react?

Sometimes our emotions take over our bodies, and we feel a little out of control. We scream at our parents when we know a quieter voice is best. We lie in our bed crying, completely unable to stop.

Let this truth comfort you: God is not afraid of our feelings.

You don't have to hide anything from God. He made you and knows how things will affect you. Even though He already knows what you are feeling, He wants you to talk to Him. Ask Him to show you what's really going on under your emotions. Why are you so angry or sad? Do you need to tell someone about it? Ask Him to heal your broken heart so that you can grieve whatever has been lost and experience joy again.

As you get ready for bed tonight, ask yourself what feelings you've felt strongly lately. Do they tend to overwhelm you? If so, tell God exactly what you're feeling. Don't be afraid to admit the negative or tough stuff. He can handle it.

Rest in that.

God, thank You for listening to me. Thank You for understanding me. Will You help me sleep peacefully tonight and wake up feeling rested?

When You're Bored

I don't say this out of need, for I have learned to be content in whatever circumstances I find myself.—PHILIPPIANS 4:11

When someone tells you to rest, does it ever feel like a punishment? Maybe resting in your mind equals being bored. Maybe it means having to be still when you don't want to. Maybe it means having to be quiet when you have so much to say. Or maybe it means having to disconnect from your phone or device, which feels like disconnecting from everyone and everything!

Instead of immediately thinking about how you'll be bored if you rest, start thinking about the things you can be grateful for as you rest.

Pay attention to what's around you. Notice the people. Look out the window and admire the trees, the birds, and the flowers. What are you grateful for in each of those?

Resting doesn't always mean sleeping. Sometimes it means being a little more quiet and a little more still so your mind and heart can refuel. When you rest, you can get creative.

Make up a new game or draw for a few minutes. Use the quiet around you to dream up new ideas. If you focus on being bored, you'll be bitter about things you can't do. But if you focus on the simple things around you, you'll learn to celebrate what you have.

This celebration of what you have is called being *content*. It's an invitation to be grateful and quiet. The next time you're bored or don't want to rest, ask God to show you all that you have, and choose a thankful heart instead of a restless one.

Rest in that.

God, would You help me to be grateful for what I have instead of being bitter or bored? Would You help me to see rest as a gift?

JOURNALING PAGES

What kind of things do you worry about when it comes to your friends or making new friends?

What kind of Friend is God to you?

DAY 31

When There's Too Much to Get Done

Whatever you do, do it from the heart, as something done for the Lord and not for people, knowing that you will receive the reward of an inheritance from the Lord. You serve the Lord Christ.—COLOSSIANS 3:23–24

No matter how easy school comes to you, homework can be stressful. Some days you have plenty of time to get the work done, and other days you have dance class, your brother's baseball game, and a giant project due the next day. You wonder how you will get it all done.

This overwhelmed feeling can leave us anxious—paralyzed, trying to figure out what to do next—and wide awake at night. In fact, I felt that when writing this book. It has brought so much joy to my life, but knowing I had to meet deadlines left me worried about my time and fearing I couldn't get everything done.

These moments are going to come and go in our lives, so the best thing to do when they happen is figure out the next step to take. Pause for a moment. Stop thinking about *all* the things you need to do. Instead identify one best next step, and do that. Then, trust God with the step after that, and the step after that. Ultimately, God is not concerned with how many things you checked off of your to-do list. He's more concerned with your attitude and your faithfulness while you do them.

Also, always ask for help when you need it! A teacher, a parent, or a friend can help you figure out what to do next and remind you of what matters along the way.

I pray before I write each one of these devotions. I want these words to be from God and not from my own head. I want my time to be spent wisely, and I want to trust that He will work through me. In the end, all our work—every step of it—belongs to Him.

Rest in that.

God, sometimes there's so much to get done that I feel stressed out. Will You help me trust You with it? Will You help me take the next best step, and remind me that it all belongs to You?

When the News Is Scary

Do not be conquered by evil, but conquer evil with good.
—ROMANS 12:21

Do you often listen to the news? Where do you get your news from? Do your parents talk about the news a lot, or do they tend to avoid it? The news keeps us informed about what's going on in our city, our country, and the world, but sometimes it's scary to hear news stories. While there's plenty of good news to share, our attention usually goes to the unsettling stories, and leaves us wondering, *What if that happens to me?*

It's okay to turn the news off.

If the stories are too hard to watch, you don't have to watch them. We want to be aware of what's going around us while not being shut down by it all. The truth is, our world is a broken place, and unfortunately, there is always going to be bad news. Jesus said, "You will have suffering in this world." But in the very next sentence, He said, "Be courageous! I have conquered the world" (John 16:33). Because we know Jesus, we will *always* have good news.

So the next time you are scared because of something you see on the news, do two things: (1) Pray, asking God for peace because He's with you. Also pray for the individuals who are part of the story, that God would help them. (2) Consider what you can do to bring good news (Jesus!) to people around you. Can you make a card for someone to encourage them? Can you bake some cookies for a neighbor to brighten their day? Can you talk about Jesus with a friend who may not know He loves them?

The world is a dark place, but Jesus is the Light (John 1:5). We get to be a light in a dark world, because Jesus is the Light in us. Scary news cannot put our light out.

Rest in that.

Jesus, You are the Light of the world. When I become overwhelmed by the news, remind me that Your Light is brighter than the darkness, and the darkness will not win.

When Your Friends Don't Get You

Am I now trying to persuade people, or God? Or am I striving to please people? If I were still trying to please people, I would not be a servant of Christ.—GALATIANS 1:10

You're at a sleepover for your friend's birthday party, and everyone's talking about their favorite TV show. You realize you've never seen it, so you ask if anyone's seen the one you've been watching with your brother. They all just stare at you.

You try describing the show while your cheeks turn red and you realize no one understands what you're talking about—or seems to care. They've started discussing other things already. As the night goes on, this kind of thing keeps happening. They're excited about a song you've never heard; you want to talk about the play you're going to be in; they want to talk about cheerleading. It doesn't take long before you feel like you're surrounded by a bunch of people who don't understand you.

Having different interests and hobbies than your friends is not something to be embarrassed about. In fact, it brings new perspectives and sparkle to a friend group! It may seem like having things in common is the only way to bond with your friends, but it's not. So keep showing them who you are and what you are passionate about, and keep showing interest in what they care about too.

The Bible reminds us not to go after the approval of our friends but to live for and serve God first. If we spend our lives always trying to fit in, we'll lose sight of what God is asking us to do. Follow Him instead.

Ultimately, when you use the gifts that God has given you—whether through art, singing, or a basketball game—you're glorifying Him by being you. God will never give you that blank stare. He loves you for being who He made you to be.

Rest in that.

Thank You, God, for making me unique! Thank You for friends who are like me and friends who are not. Help me be confident in how You made me and learn from friends who are different from me.

When You're Lost in a Crowd

The LORD your God is among you, a warrior who saves.
—ZEPHANIAH 3:17

A while back, I went on a mission trip really far away from my family—like oceans away—with a lot of people I didn't know well. Without my friends, family, and familiar surroundings, I was really lonely at first.

We tend to describe lonely moments as those when we're alone in our room and don't want to be, or when we've asked people to hang out but they're all busy. The truth is, loneliness can hit you when you're at a crowded lunch table, at a birthday party, or on a trip with people who don't know you well, like I was.

I took a journal with me on that trip, and instead of writing down my thoughts, I started writing down Bible verses that helped me remember I wasn't alone. I would read them over and over while I was gone, and you know what? They still come to mind even now when I'm feeling lonely. Here are a few of them:

"The LORD your God is among you, a warrior who saves. He will rejoice over you with gladness. He will be quiet in his love. He will delight in you with singing." (Zephaniah 3:17)

"Be strong and courageous; don't be terrified or afraid of them. For the LORD your God is the one who will go with you; he will not leave you or abandon you." (Deuteronomy 31:6)

"If God is for us, who is against us?" (Romans 8:31)

If you are ever feeling lonely, try writing down Bible verses that will help you remember what's true. Loneliness is real, but God is real too. He is with you. Always. You are never alone. And even if you feel like you're getting lost in a crowd, God sees you.

Rest in that.

God, thank You for always being with me and never leaving me by myself. I love You and ask that when I am feeling lonely, You will remind me that You are right there.

DAY 35

When You Can't Sleep

Cast your burden on the LORD, and he will sustain you; he will never allow the righteous to be shaken. —PSALM 55:22

I'm not tired."

How many times have you said that when it's time to go to bed? You lay your head down on your pillow and stare at the ceiling, eyes wide open. Maybe you try reading a book. Or listening to music. Or watching a show. But none of those things work; you're still not tired. And as the clock ticks, the worry wheel starts to spin. *What if I never fall asleep? What if I have to do my full day tomorrow on no sleep at all?*

Our minds can easily get way ahead of us—thinking about all that might go wrong—instead of winding down, shutting down, and drifting into sleep.

God will help us when our sleep does not. If we get little rest, God will carry us through the next day, and we'll probably fall asleep more easily the next night! So when you're not tired, choose to focus on God, the safest place to direct your thoughts. Pray as you calm your mind. Take some deep breaths to relax your body.

God can give you rest, *and* He can give you energy on days when you're sleepy. He's that powerful. He never needs sleep—that's how powerful He is (Psalm 121:4)! There's nothing too complicated for Him. Isn't that incredible? You can relax, close your eyes, talk to Him, and shut out the idea that you're never going to fall asleep. You can rest.

Rest in that.

Thank You, God, for helping me sleep and giving me strength and energy. Would You help sleep come easily tonight?

DAY 36

When You Feel Too Young

Don't let anyone despise your youth, but set an example for the believers in speech, in conduct, in love, in faith, and in purity.—1 TIMOTHY 4:12

Have you ever run up to a roller coaster to get in line to ride it then realize you're not tall enough? You stand there watching everyone have fun and wish you could be part of it.

You may be past the days of being turned away from rides, but I bet there are things you wish you were old enough to do but can't yet. Feeling left out can leave us feeling unseen and unimportant. Especially if it's because we're too young.

Let me remind you: You are smart. Your thoughts matter. We need you.

Don't let the things you can't do yet keep you up at night. And don't let the things you can't do yet keep you from doing what you can do now.

Jesus always has a way of seeing people others tended to overlook. Have you ever heard the song about Zacchaeus, the wee, little man? Because he was short, he climbed up in a tree so he could see Jesus over the crowd of people around him (Luke 19:1–10). When we sing that song, we can get caught up in how short Zacchaeus was and forget the whole point of the story! Jesus picked him out of the crowd and told Zacchaeus He wanted to go to his house.

This wasn't the first or last time Jesus paid special attention to someone in a crowd when everyone else was ignoring them (Mark 5:25–29; Mark 10:46–52). Jesus does not overlook what He made, no matter how seemingly insignificant others think that person is. This means Jesus does not overlook you even when others do. What if you viewed yourself the way Jesus did?

More than that, what if you viewed other people the way Jesus did? Do not let your size or age affect how you act. Let people see Jesus through you.

Rest in that.

God, thank You for always seeing me when I don't feel old enough, big enough, or loud enough to be noticed. Would You help me do big things for You even while I'm still young?

DAY 37

When You've Got the First-Time Jitters

"Peace I leave with you. My peace I give to you. I do not give to you as the world gives. Don't let your heart be troubled or fearful."—JOHN 14:27

Do you get the first-day-of-school jitters? You start counting down the days until school starts, thinking about what you're going to wear, who will be in your class, what you'll eat for lunch, and where your desk will be.

You're both nervous and excited, and the jitters leave you tossing and turning. Even if it's not the first day of school you're thinking about, there are lots of "firsts" in life that can get us all worked up. Your first volleyball game. Your first band practice. Your first time going on a trip without your parents.

There's something we can ask God for every time a "first" moment is approaching: peace.

The Bible calls Jesus the Prince of Peace (Isaiah 9:6), so not only can He give us peace, but He Himself is peace. Ask for peace for your mind as you think about all the new experiences coming up. Ask for peace for your heart as you make new friends at school or church. Ask for peace for your body as you walk through the doors of your gym or step on the bus.

And remember that Jesus also had "firsts." The Bible says that Jesus became fully man when He left heaven (Philippians 2:7), which means He had to learn everything like we do and experience it like we do—for the first time! Jesus can be our peace because He knows what it's like to be human. He's walked our road perfectly, and He can help us navigate it.

Rest in that.

God, I'm both excited and nervous. Will You give me peace and remind me that You've gone before me? Thank You, Jesus!

When You Need Help But Don't Want to Ask

"I do not call you servants anymore, because a servant doesn't know what his master is doing. I have called you friends, because I have made known to you everything I have heard from my Father."—JOHN 15:15

When you're having a hard time with a math problem or can't figure out your science homework, is it easy for you to ask for help? I hope your answer is yes! If it's not easy, though, let's talk about that for a second, because that was me (and sometimes still is).

Asking for help means having the attention put on me, which I don't like. It also means admitting that I don't understand the assignment or question like everyone else seems to.

The truth is, the longer we stay in our heads and worry about what people will think if we ask for help, the longer we delay solving the problem. Your teachers, your friends, your parents . . . they all want to help! And so often, they find joy in coming alongside you.

God designed us to live our lives with other people, not alone. He knew we'd need each other! That's why after God created Adam, He created Eve. Genesis 2:18 tells us, "The Lord God said, 'It is not good for the man to be alone. I will make a helper corresponding to him.'"

More than that: for every moment you're anxious about asking that question in class, I'd bet someone else has that same question. So when you take the step to ask for help, you're giving your friends and classmates permission to do the same. They'll follow your lead!

The people in your life—your parents, siblings, classmates, friends, and teachers—are a gift from God. Be honest. Let them in on what you need, and in return, be the daughter, sister, classmate, and friend they need as well.

Rest in that.

God, thank You for teachers, parents, and friends who help me when I'm stuck! Would You show me when I need to let people in and help me to be honest with them?

When You're in a Fight

My dear brothers and sisters, understand this: Everyone should be quick to listen, slow to speak, and slow to anger.
—JAMES 1:19

I don't like when people are mad at me, and I don't like being in an argument with someone. The older I've gotten, the better I've learned to navigate conflict, but if I was in a fight with someone at your age, it would stick with me for days. I would go back over everything that was said (or not said) in my head and try to figure out what could have gone differently. Sometimes this would keep me up at night.

When's the last time you were in an argument with someone? Was it over something small, like who gets to sit in the best seat in the car? Or was it over something bigger, like who is going to confess to the teacher that you and your friend cheated on the assignment?

Thankfully, we don't have to wonder and stress over how to deal with conflict because the Bible helps us with that. Today's verse from James 1, for example, reminds us to be:

1. quick to listen;

2. slow to speak; and

3. slow to anger.

In your most recent argument, did any of these come easily to you? Which one was the hardest? How might you remember to listen first and be slow to anger the next time you're in an argument? It's not easy to do, but did you know that the Holy Spirt, who lives in you, can help you with this?

When the heat is rising in the room, ask the Holy Spirit to help you stay calm, open your ears to listen, and bite your tongue (figuratively, of course). God knew we couldn't do this on our own, so He gives us the Holy Spirit to help.

Rest in that.

God, it's not easy to listen, be slow to speak, and remain calm when I get mad at someone. Will You help me? Will You show me how to control my anger?

DAY 40

When You Are Trying to Be Like Them

"I know the plans I have for you"—this is the LORD's declaration—"plans for your well-being, not for disaster, to give you a future and a hope."—JEREMIAH 29:11

I remember a time in my life when I was always known as "Adam's sister." Thankfully, I really looked up to my brother, so it was a compliment to be known as his little sister. But there was always the pressure to be as well-liked and respected as he was. He was the fun one. Everybody's friend. I was shyer, more reserved. Could I be everyone's friend too?

It's easy to compare ourselves to our siblings. Whether they're older or younger, we can get caught up in competing for good grades, performing as well as they do, or attracting the kind of attention they do.

But God has a plan that's just for you. It's not the exact same plan as He has for your brother or your sister. It's as unique as you are.

God has given you a distinct personality and your own special set of talents; He created you to be your own person. So cheer on your brothers and sisters. Encourage them. Be supportive. Then walk confidently in who God created you to be.

Let go of the worry that you won't be like your siblings because the world doesn't need you to be them. The world needs you to be you! It needs your smart, kind, talented self. God made you in His image, which means you are the exact reflection of Him that He wanted to make. And that's enough.

Turns out, Adam and I ended up living in the same town as adults. Now sometimes he meets people that say, "Hey, you're Katy's brother!" and we just smile, because he's proud of me, and I'm proud of him. God is delighted when you cheer your siblings on, no matter how old you are.

Rest in that.

Thank You, God, for siblings! Thank You for reminding me that I can just be me and not try to be like anyone else. I love the way You made me!

JOURNALING PAGES

When do you feel lonely? Include any times you've felt that way recently.

What helps you when you feel lonely? Make a list of those things and thank God for them as you write!

When You're Worried About Having What You Need

My God will supply all your needs according to his riches in glory in Christ Jesus.—PHILIPPIANS 4:19

So much of your life right now is about transitions. Transitioning from one grade to another, transitioning from one dance class to another, moving into middle school, taking on new responsibilities at home and school, and more.

The change is fun and exciting, but when classes get harder and you're responsible for more, it can get a little overwhelming. You might start to wonder if you can handle it all, if you have what it takes, and if you have all you need.

Can I tell you about how God shows up over and over again and provides exactly what you need in the moment?

In the book of Exodus in the Bible, the Israelites wandered in the desert for a really long time, waiting to be taken to the land they were promised. Can you imagine how many times they asked, "Are we there yet?"

Day after day, God provided exactly what the Israelites needed to help them get through. He literally made it rain bread for them (Exodus 16:4).

And God will give you what you need too. You can ask Him for confidence as you enter middle school, for new friends when you join a new team, or for steadiness as you advance a level in gymnastics. Some days you may need something physical—for a stomachache to go away or your eyes to quit itching from allergies. Other days you may need something for your heart—a joyful reminder or help calming your nerves. God shows up over and over again with exactly what we need.

Sometimes He even shows up with something unexpected— something we didn't know we needed! God has a big plan, and we can rest in knowing that He will provide one way or another. He is good.

Rest in that.

Thank You, God, for letting me come to You and ask for what I need. It makes me grateful to know that as things change, the older I get, You will provide.

DAY 42

When You're Trying to Stay Out of Trouble

Do not be conformed to this age, but be transformed by the renewing of your mind, so that you may discern what is the good, pleasing, and perfect will of God.—ROMANS 12:2

How easily are your friends able to persuade you to do something you know you shouldn't do? Peer pressure is tricky, and it can keep us up at night. You want to stand up for yourself and what you believe. But you also don't want to miss out on everything your friends are doing!

Sometimes it can feel like we're choosing between what our parents and other adults want for us (safety) and what our friends or other peers want us to do (adventure). In every situation, we have to decide what is wise. Remember, there are many experiences you and your friends will have that can be both safe *and* adventurous. Others might seem fun at first but can be dangerous or even disobedient.

So, how do we know what's wise?

The Bible tells us to choose God's way over the world's way, and we can figure out God's way by staying close to Him. Memorize verses from the Bible about wisdom. Pray, asking God to make your decision clear. Talk to other Christians who trust in God and know His Word. God also gave us the Holy Spirit, His Helper, to nudge us when we're getting off track and making bad decisions. Trust Him.

In the book of Genesis, God told Adam and Eve they could eat fruit from any of the gorgeous trees in the garden of Eden except for one. Did they listen? Nope, and there were life-changing consequences. God was very clear with His instructions, and He's very clear with us as well. We don't have to guess what's right and wrong because He's laid it out for us in the Bible. We can trust that God's way is better than the world's way.

Rest in that.

God, when I'm tempted to make a bad decision, would You continue to nudge me and remind me of what's right? I want to live for You and not this world!

When You're Not Sure If God Can Hear You

Draw near to God, and he will draw near to you. Cleanse your hands, sinners, and purify your hearts, you double-minded.—JAMES 4:8

Have you ever been on a video chat and your internet starts going out? Suddenly your face is frozen on the screen or your words sound choppy, and your friends and classmates are staring at you, confused.

"Can you hear me?"

You're practically yelling at the screen, yet everyone on the other side can't hear a thing.

Sometimes it seems like the same thing when we're talking to God. Maybe He hasn't answered a prayer request you've made for years, or perhaps you feel like one bad thing is happening after another in your life. You're left wondering if you and God have a good connection. "Hello, God? Am I muted?" you ask.

The Bible tells us that if we come near to God, He'll come near to us. Now, that may seem confusing, because we can't physically see God. So, how do we come near to Him? Imagine He's sitting there next to you. Pray. Talk to Him and tell Him why you're thankful for Him. Ask Him for what you need. Trust that He hears every word.

You don't have to rely on a Wi-Fi connection or phone to know God or pray! He always hears you. God may not answer your prayer the way you thought He would, but He always has a bigger plan in mind. If He's not sharing that plan with you, open your Bible. Read about His promises, and hear what He told His people about His plans for them.

If we feel like we can't hear God, we don't have to wonder what He has in mind for us. We have an entire Bible full of His words. Read them. Pray them. God will draw near to you as you do so.

Rest in that.

God, You are good. Thank You for giving me a reminder of who You are and what You have for me through the Bible. Please help me remember You always hear me when I feel like we're disconnected.

DAY 44

When Your Heart Hurts

Blessed be the God and Father of our Lord Jesus Christ, the Father of mercies and the God of all comfort. He comforts us in all our affliction, so that we may be able to comfort those who are in any kind of affliction, through the comfort we ourselves receive from God.—2 CORINTHIANS 1:3–4

What does being sad typically look like for you? Do you get really quiet? Are you quick to cry, or do you hold your tears back? Do you tend to get upset easily?

Maybe no one has ever told you this before: it's okay to be sad.

Some days, the reality of what's going on around you will be too much. Your heart will be so heavy that it hurts, and all you can think about is the sadness. You can't focus on school. You can't fall asleep. Maybe you aren't even excited to see your friends.

Today's verse reminds us something that's true of God: He's a God of all comfort. This means that on the days when everything is sad and when your heart is heavy, you can lean on Him to give you comfort.

Think about Jesus. The Bible tell us He was well acquainted with pain and sorrow (Isaiah 53:3). While He was on earth, He cried (John 11:35). He knew sadness. Your hurt isn't a mystery to Him. Jesus knows what your sadness is, and He knows what sadness feels like.

You can also let someone else know you're sad. They may not be able to fix everything, but they can help you not feel so alone when your heart hurts. Sometimes the greatest gift is just having someone else to sit with you or listen.

Being sad is not a weakness; otherwise, Jesus would have been weak! Sadness is just an emotion we will feel from time to time, and that's okay. Sadness reminds us that this world is not what it should be; it reminds us that we need God. We have a God who comforts and heals. Lean on Him in your sadness because He can carry you. His power is greater than your tears.

Rest in that.

Thank You for helping me when I feel sad, God. It brings me comfort to know You're in control when it feels like everything is out of control.

DAY 45

When You Don't Know How to Be a Good Friend

Encourage one another and build each other up as you are already doing.—1 THESSALONIANS 5:11

My friends and I have a tradition on New Year's Day where we get together to talk about the previous year and dream and pray about the next. My favorite part, though, is when we take a few minutes to encourage one another. We tell each person the good things we see in them and what we hope God does for them in the next year. We get to say things like, "I'm so proud of you," "I love the way you just kept trusting God when things were so hard," and "Here's how I want to pray for you this year . . ."

It's special because it sets us up for a new year feeling encouraged, loved, and seen instead of worried and anxious about the future.

Finding good friends can be a challenge, but being a good friend doesn't have to be.

As you make new friends, be the kind of friend that encourages other people. Be loyal and trustworthy. That kind of person is someone people want to be around! If you don't see this kind of behavior within your group of friends, be the first one to start it. Compliment your friend on what she's good at. Tell her why you like being her friend. Invite her over to your house to hang out.

Jesus is the perfect example of a good friend. He showed compassion. He listened. He was focused on others and not distracted. He spent quality time with His friends! So on the days when you're worried about being a good friend, look at the way Jesus lived. We can learn something from His kindness and love for others.

Jesus is our greatest Friend, and letting your friends see His Spirit shine through you is the best gift you can give them.

Rest in that.

Would You help me see people and love people the way You do, Jesus? Would You help me be a good friend?

DAY 46

When You're Not Sure If Things Will Get Better

May the God of hope fill you with all joy and peace as you believe so that you may overflow with hope by the power of the Holy Spirit.—ROMANS 15:13

Do you know those weeks when one thing after another keeps going wrong? It feels like a giant ball pit that you jump in, sink to the bottom, and can't crawl your way out of.

One day you get a bad grade, the next day your mom has a scary diagnosis at the doctor, and the next day your best friend says she found a new best friend. It's hard to find the good in anything when all you feel is bad. I've been there.

Today, we're looking at Romans 15:13. The book of Romans was written by Paul, who definitely knew what it was like to have one thing after the other go wrong. Paul spent a lot of his ministry locked up in jail because people weren't happy that he was talking about Jesus. Do you know what he did while he was in jail, though? He kept praying, he kept worshiping God, and he kept talking about Jesus. He knew where true hope comes from. It comes from God, not from our circumstances.

We can't know if one bad thing might come after another, but we can change the way we think about the bad things. Just as Paul chose to have hope on the hard days, you can too! And this isn't an empty, take-a-chance kind of hope. We have hope because we've watched God fulfill every promise He's ever made in the Bible and know that in the end, He wins! Our hope is not in bad things stopping now. It's in Jesus getting rid of the bad things forever, when He decides to.

Until that day comes, we still have God here with us. The Holy Spirit lives in you and can give you the peace and hope you need to get through each day—whatever it brings.

Rest in that.

I trust You with all this, God. I trust You.

DAY 47

When You're Scared at School

"Haven't I commanded you: be strong and courageous? Do not be afraid or discouraged, for the LORD your God is with you wherever you go."—JOSHUA 1:9

Have you ever hoped a fire drill or tornado drill would happen right before your math test so you wouldn't have to take it? Maybe that's just me! I would accept any interruption necessary to get out of taking a test.

There are so many school drills you have to practice these days. While it may mean getting out of class for a few minutes, your stomach might do a few turns when you imagine a fire actually burning down the building!

We practice these drills for the same reason we practice our multiplication tables and spelling. We do them so when we need them, our response comes naturally. We know exactly what to do and how to do it.

It all can be a little bit scary, though. There are so many what-if? questions that can leave you feeling unsafe when going to school. So here's what I want you to do: Just as you would do a drill to prepare for an earthquake, practice memorizing verses from the Bible to prepare for those scary moments. Look for verses related to fear, and meditate on the words.

When we memorize what the Bible says, we can rely on God's truth when we're afraid. You can say these in your head:

God is with me wherever I go. (Joshua 1:9)

God will strengthen me and help me. (Isaiah 41:10)

God is coming to my rescue. (Isaiah 35:4)

We cannot prevent fires, tornadoes, earthquakes, or other disasters. These things are out of our hands. What we can do is trust that God is always with us, and when disasters come, He will help us through.

Rest in that.

Thank You, God, for always being with me and always helping me be strong. Will You help me not focus on what I can't control but on Your Word instead?

DAY 48

When You're Overwhelmed

After these events, the word of the LORD came to Abram in a vision: "Do not be afraid, Abram. I am your shield; your reward will be very great."—GENESIS 15:1

When you have an overwhelming amount of schoolwork, how does it make you feel? Maybe you're struggling to understand something new in your science class and you have a big test coming up that you're scared about. Maybe you don't know how to do a project you've been assigned. Or maybe every class has too much homework this week.

Does having loads to do make you want to give up? Do you feel like you don't even want to try?

When you get overwhelmed, you might feel like anything and everything is too much. Your mom may ask you to clean your room, and you snap back at her that you can't (when all it would take is five minutes of folding your clothes). Your friend may ask you to help her with something after school, and you cry because the very thought of stopping what you have to do to help someone else is too much.

I love what today's verse says about God being our shield. Can you picture that? You're standing in a battle, and as things are flying at you, trying to knock you down, God is the shield. He's the barrier protecting you and helping you to stay standing.

It may not look like it all the time, but we are all in a battle every day. Things are being thrown at us from all directions, and God is the shield who helps us remain standing. So don't sit down in the middle of the battle. Don't turn your back and walk away. Most importantly, don't lay down the shield, forgetting about God. Trust that He will help you keep fighting, no matter what comes your way.

Rest in that.

God, thank You for being my shield. Thank You for helping me stand up when I feel like I just want to fall down.

DAY 49

When You Have a Lot of Questions

I will stand at my guard post and station myself on the lookout tower. I will watch to see what he will say to me and what I should reply about my complaint.—HABAKKUK 2:1

Like all kids, your brain is probably full of questions. You have questions about how the world works. You have questions about God. Maybe questions about what's going to happen this coming year. Perhaps questions about why certain things happened in the past.

God is not scared of all the questions you have. In fact, He welcomes them!

Following God requires trust, but it doesn't mean we won't have questions along the way. God works in big ways that our little minds sometimes can't understand. (This is true for adults too.) You can ask God anything you want to. The best resource we have is the Bible, God's Word. We find a ton of answers and examples when we read the Bible. Don't be intimidated by how long it is! It's full of stories of how God kept His word, God's purpose for our lives, and what He's promised for all the days ahead.

You won't find every answer to every question in the Bible, but you will discover what God has chosen to reveal about Himself, humanity, and life itself. The more you study it, the more truth you'll discover—just ask any adult who's been a Christian for a long time!

So as you grow up and have more questions, don't let those questions keep you from getting to know God. Bring them all to Him—your questions about the world, your future, and your family. We get to rest in the fact that even if we don't get an answer, God has a plan. As we see in the Bible, God has never failed, and He won't fail us either.

Rest in that.

God, thank You for never getting annoyed by all my questions. Thank You for loving me even when I doubt You.

When Taking a Test

I lift my eyes toward the mountains. Where will my help come from? My help comes from the LORD, the Maker of heaven and earth.—PSALM 121:1–2

What do you think about standardized tests? I was never a fan. The pressure, the long instructions, the prep work needed—it always felt like such an intimidating day! When the classroom got quiet, and the teacher finished reading out those long test-taking instructions, I was left with letters swirling on a page, a hundred multiple-choice answer bubbles to fill in, and a racing heart. Could I pass the test?

Some test days aren't as intense as that, but there's always something coming that you have to prepare for—a spelling test, memorizing multiplication tables, studying the capitals of each state. While you may have someone to study with, when test day arrives, it's all in your hands (or should I say in your brain?).

It can be a lonely and unsettling feeling to be given harder tests and more responsibility as you grow up. The more homework that piles up, the more you wonder how to get it all done. You can't bring your mom with you, so will you get by on your own?

Take a look at today's verse. Even though growing up means doing more and more things on your own (which is also exciting!), you never truly have to get by on your own because God is with you. When you're taking a hard test, ask God to calm your heart and mind so you can recall the things you studied. Also, ask Him to remind you that a test is just a test; it's not your life. Ask Him for peace and the right perspective so that you can give it your best.

When you rely on God to help you, you will realize quickly that big responsibility is less scary because you know you are not alone.

Rest in that.

God, thank You for always helping me. It helps me calm down to know that You are always with me even as I'm given more responsibilities. What a gift!

What's the hardest thing about school for you right now?

What helps you remember God is with you when you're at school?

_____

_____

_____

_____

_____

_____

_____

_____

_____

_____

_____

_____

DAY 51

When Your Friends Leave

When David had finished speaking with Saul, Jonathan was bound to David in close friendship, and loved him as much as he loved himself.—1 Samuel 18:1

I had a best friend named Caitlin when I was in the fourth grade, and we were pretty much inseparable. Together, we shared countless sleepovers, bike rides around the neighborhood, and stories about *NSYNC and the Backstreet Boys.

When she told me her family was moving to another state, I was crushed. Our parents assured us we could visit and write letters to each other, but who would be my in-person best friend?

When friendships change, it can be easy to think you will never make another good friend. That the friendship is over forever. You don't know that yet, though, do you? Friendships will come and go, and some will last our entire lives. So, what if in those moments of change, instead of assuming the worst, you trust God with the plan for your friendship? What if you pray for your friends instead?

First Samuel tells us the story of two friends, David and Jonathan. Jonathan's dad, King Saul, was afraid of David and wanted to kill him (1 Samuel 19:11–12). For his own safety, David had to leave, and Jonathan helped him escape (1 Samuel 20). Don't you think Jonathan missed his friend once he was gone? How sad! But he trusted God's plan for David and knew their friendship could withstand the change.

When we remember to trust God even with our friendships, it helps us get through the hard seasons of change—the sadness and loneliness and even anger. God has a plan for both you and your friend, and when she leaves, it doesn't mean God won't take care of both of you. It's okay to be sad. But also, don't stop asking how you might still show her love after she moves. Most importantly, don't underestimate what God can do with your friendships, no matter how far away you live from one another.

Rest in that.

God, thank You for friends! Thank You for the joy they bring me and the way they make me laugh. Will You help me trust You when my friends move? I love You!

DAY 52

When You're Not Sure What's True

The entirety of your word is truth, each of your righteous judgments endures forever.—PSALM 119:160

How do you feel about true-or-false questions on tests? I can remember staring at each statement and trying to weigh which one I was the most certain about. It made my head hurt.

Example: True or False? The sky is green.

Okay, obviously, this one is false. But sometimes, answers just aren't that clear! Beyond taking tests, we often have to figure out what's true and what's not in life. When you hear stories from friends and wonder if they're true—or you are not sure who to believe when you hear two different things about the same situation—it can get confusing!

How do you figure out what's true when it doesn't feel clear? Simple. You ask questions!

There's so much information being thrown at you—from school, from friends, from home, from the internet—that it can leave you with a lot of questions. Even if you're nervous, don't be afraid to ask. Don't be afraid to open your Bible and see what God says or talk to a parent or teacher to help you figure it out.

Unfortunately, the devil would prefer to confuse us and keep us distracted. It's his favorite game because when we're confused, we easily take our eyes off Jesus and start believing things that aren't true.

But God is not a God of confusion (1 Corinthians 14:33). He's clear, and He's given us instructions to live by in the Bible. Ask Him to help you figure out what's true. Read your Bible and memorize verses so you can compare the truth of what it says to things you hear.

You have what you need because God has given you Himself, His Word, and people to help you find out what's true.

Rest in that.

God, things can get really confusing sometimes, but I am so thankful You help me figure out what's real and true!

DAY 53

When Following the Rules Is Hard

He is our God, and we are the people of his pasture, the sheep under his care.—PSALM 95:7

Does it ever feel like you're surrounded by a lot of rules? You have rules at school, rules in your art class, rules on the field, and rules at home. Does following the rules come easily to you, or is it a challenge?

There will always be moments when we want to do whatever we want without thinking about the rules. We want to jump in the pool even though it's closed for cleaning. We want to stay up past our bedtime reading a good book. We want to watch the show our parents said is off limits.

Some days you may not understand the rules, and your parents may tell you to follow them, just because they said so. This can be irritating. But these rules and guidelines on your life have a purpose.

The Bible often compares humans to sheep. I hate to break it you, but sheep aren't known for being super smart. This is why they need a shepherd to watch over them. This is why they have a fence to keep them contained. Without those things, they wander, get lost, and risk being hurt or eaten by another animal.

Rules and boundaries keep us contained and help protect us too. We may not see them that way—because it may feel like all they're doing is keeping us from having fun—but the truth is, they prevent us from getting hurt.

Rest in the fact that your parents, teachers, coaches, and God have put rules in place to help you grow and keep you safe. Your Shepherd, God, especially has your best interests in mind. He knows exactly what you need.

Rest in that.

God, when following the rules feels hard, will You remind me why the rules matter? Would You help me obey with a good attitude and trust those in charge?

When You Keep Messing Up

He said to me, "My grace is sufficient for you, for my power is perfected in weakness."—2 CORINTHIANS 12:9

Have you ever been working on a math problem for so long that your pencil eraser wears down to nearly nothing? You stop, erase, and start over so many times because you can't seem to get it right. Maybe your eyes start welling up with tears because you're frustrated or because you're far behind your classmates. Or maybe you're ready to rip up your paper and give up altogether.

We carry these heavy feelings around when it comes to sin too. A simple mistake may be easy to correct next time, but sometimes we struggle with something over and over again. Recognizing these sins can keep us wide awake at night wondering how to change (and how to fall asleep!).

First of all, as soon as you realize you've done something wrong, name it and agree with God that it is sin. Then ask for forgiveness. Pray to God for forgiveness, and go to the person you've hurt (or disobeyed) for forgiveness. Figure out a plan that will guard you from the temptation to do the same thing again. Finally, let it rest with God.

God has given us grace, a gift we did not deserve. Grace is like jumping into a deep swimming pool and feeling the weight go away as you float back to the top. Through God's grace, He takes your guilt and shame and carries it for you so you can swim through life without that sinking feeling about your sin. And God will never quit doing that for you. He will never stop showing you grace.

That may seem like a crazy idea—that He wouldn't ever give up on us—but God's grace, unlike a pencil eraser, never runs out.

Rest in that.

God, I'm so sorry I do some things I know are wrong over and over again. Will You forgive me? Thank You for never, ever giving up on me. I love You!

DAY 55

When You Have to Decide

One who isolates himself pursues selfish desires; he rebels against all sound wisdom.—PROVERBS 18:1

When it comes time to make a decision, how do you do it? Do you just go with your gut? Do you ask someone else what they think? Do you search for an answer on Google?

Decisions can be downright overwhelming, and they can keep us up at night! Deciding whether to stick with dance or soccer, choosing which birthday party to go to when they both fall on the same day, and even deciding what to wear—it can all be hard. But God did not ask us to make decisions by figuring them out alone. God makes Himself and all of His wisdom available to us when we read His words in the Bible and when we pray (James 1:5). So ask God for help when making a decision!

You can also learn more about what good decisions look like when reading the Bible. For example, Proverbs is called a book of wisdom because the wisest man who had ever lived wrote it (1 Kings 10:23). The book of Job shows us how to handle suffering, and the book of James is about wise living.

Every book of the Bible helps us grow in wisdom because "all Scripture is inspired by God and is profitable for teaching, for rebuking, for correcting, for training in righteousness, so that the man of God may be complete, equipped for every good work" (2 Timothy 3:16–17).

But what if you make a bad decision? What if you make a foolish choice? God will not walk away from you. He will still be there to help you learn and grow.

Rest in that.

Thank You for always being available to talk, God. Sometimes I don't know what to do. Thank You for helping me make decisions!

DAY 56

When to Pray

I want the men in every place to pray, lifting up holy hands without anger or argument.—1 TIMOTHY 2:8

It never fails. When I get mad about something, I go to the first person who will listen and start venting about it. I spill all the details, waiting for them to feel bad for me, get mad along with me, and make it all better for me.

But whoever I'm venting to can't fix everything. And so, the cycle continues. I talk to every friend or family member about the thing I'm mad about, as if I've shaken up a giant soda bottle, taken the cap off, and let it spew all over the place—drenching everything and everyone around me.

It's typically about a week later that I realize I never talked to God about it. I never prayed. I never told *Him* why I was angry or asked Him for help.

We can spend so much energy retelling the story to our friends and family, or on getting worked up in our heads, that we forget to tell the one Person who can actually handle our problem. It never fails: as soon as I start praying about whatever is wrong, the anger and other emotions start to settle. This doesn't mean the issue is immediately resolved, but He always gives an invitation to rest. When we pray to God about whatever makes us mad, it's also our moment to give ourselves back to Him.

What's bothering you this week? Have you talked to God about it? He's bigger and better than any other option because He knows you and your heart completely. He knows what you've been through and what's still to come. So the next time you're upset, pray first and talk to people second. It will change everything.

Rest in that.

God, will You help me remember to bring everything to You? When I'm tempted to ask for everyone else's help except Yours, will You remind me You're there?

When Everything Is Too Loud

"Don't let your heart be troubled. Believe in God; believe also in me."—JOHN 14:1

When's the last time you attended a concert? (Or maybe you haven't gotten to yet!) I love live music, so going to concerts is one of my favorite things to do. It's so much fun to see the musicians on stage doing what they love and enjoying the songs with everyone else in the audience!

But concerts are loud. That's obvious when you try to tell your friend that you see someone you know in the crowd, or when you answer your phone and have to plug your other ear and yell, but they don't always hear you!

Does your mind ever feel this loud? Sometimes problems are swirling around in our minds so much—worries about our schoolwork or our friends or our families—that our thoughts get so loud we can't possibly hear or understand ourselves.

When this happens, here's an idea: Find a quiet place—in your room, under a tree outside, on your porch—and sit in silence for a while. It might feel weird or uncomfortable, but just give it a minute! Consider writing down what's going through your head. The physical act of putting thoughts on paper can help the loud, jumbly mess inside your head become something you can let go of.

All the noise inside your mind doesn't have to take over your day. Spend time in the quiet, spend time with God, and bring Him the things that cause all the noise. The trouble in your heart and the trouble in your mind are not troubles to God. He can turn down the volume and bring you peace.

Rest in that.

God, would You bring quiet and peace when it feels like everything in my mind is so loud? Thank You for helping me!

DAY 58

When You Don't Know If You Can Trust God

Take delight in the LORD, and he will give you your heart's desires. Commit your way to the LORD; trust in him, and he will act, making your righteousness shine like the dawn, your justice like the noonday.—PSALM 37:4–6

Have you ever told a friend to keep a secret for you and then wondered if she actually would? Have you ever needed someone safe to talk to but weren't sure who you could trust?

People mess up. A lot. This means that they might not come through for us when we need them, and it's hard to know if it will always be that way or if they just made one mistake in the past. As we spend more time with a particular person, watch their actions, and listen to them, we begin to understand whether they are someone we can trust.

Sometimes, we begin to wonder if God is like the people around us. How do we know we can trust Him when we can't see Him? How do we know we can trust Him in those moments when everything around us feels hard and scary?

That's when we turn to the Bible, God's Word to us, to learn more about who He is and what He does.

• The book of Genesis tells us God created us and the world we live in. You can trust the One who created you (Genesis 1:1).

• God can always be trusted because He promised a Savior would come to save the world, and Jesus did (Isaiah 9:6–7).

• God can always be trusted because He gave us the Holy Spirit to live with us and be our Helper (John 14:26).

• God is a good Father. He never fails us (Romans 8:15). So we can trust Him.

• God can always be trusted because over and over in the Bible, He tells us He's going to come through for us, and He does (Joshua 21:45).

Rest in that.

I trust You, God. Thank You for always keeping Your Word. Thank You for always keeping Your promises.

DAY 59

When You're Worried You'll Oversleep

May the LORD make his face shine on you and be gracious to you.—NUMBERS 6:25

Who or what helps you wake up in the morning? Do your parents come in and tell you to get up? Do you set an alarm? Does the sun peek in your through window and the light wake you up? Whatever it may be, do you ever worry the plan will fail?

I'm an alarm girl. I set it every night (unless it's the weekend), and I rely on it to start my day off right. But there have been days when I've set the alarm for p.m. instead of a.m., or I turned it off and fell back asleep, and the chaos that followed set me up for a terrible day ahead. Some nights (usually before a big day) I can get so worried about this happening again that I can't even fall asleep.

Here's the thing: Stuff like this will happen every now and then. Even when we plan ahead and check our alarm twice, or we remind our parents we need to be up earlier than normal, something will go wrong and we'll oversleep. But you know what? It's okay! One chaotic morning won't ruin your entire life; it doesn't mean it will happen every day; and it certainly doesn't mean God has run out of grace for you.

So when you're planning for the next day, do the things you can control: set the alarm, check in with your parents, and then rest in God. If something goes wrong the next morning, take a deep breath and pray. Ask God for a reset moment and trust that He will provide it. Just as the sun rises every single morning, you can have a fresh start (even when your first start feels stressful). The Bible tells us God's mercies are new every morning (Lamentations 3:22–23). And guess what? That's true whether you wake up on time or not!

Rest in that.

God, will You calm my mind tonight as I fall asleep and help me trust that Your timing is the best timing?

When Your Family Feels Different than Everyone Else's

You received the Spirit of adoption, by whom we cry out, *"Abba*, Father!" The Spirit himself testifies together with our spirit that we are God's children, and if children, also heirs—heirs of God and coheirs with Christ.—ROMANS 8:15–17

I wish I could grab lunch with you one day and hear more about you. I want to know about what you love and who the important people are in your life.

I realize that we've talked about family from time to time in this book, and "family" means different things to each of us. Your family probably doesn't look like mine. Yours also may not look the way you imagined. Losing a family member, or parents divorcing, or having a really mean parent may leave you feeling a little lost and lonely.

So if you're wondering why your family feels different than other families, if you're waiting for a forever family, or if your heart is breaking because of a tough situation in your family, you are not alone. As a child of God, you were given both a heavenly Father and a family.

• You have been adopted by God and given a new identity in Him (John 1:12). You are a new creation (2 Corinthians 5:17).

• You have a good Father who not only loves you; He's delighted about you (Zephaniah 3:17).

• You have brothers and sisters because other followers of Jesus are your spiritual brothers and sisters (Romans 12:5).

• You are not forgotten or left out. You are not an afterthought or a plan B. You are chosen and cherished by God (Isaiah 43:1).

• You have a forever family because you will spend eternity with God and with your brothers and sisters in Christ (Romans 8:29–30).

Rest in that.

Heavenly Father, thank You for giving me a family. Thank You for loving me and adopting me. I am your daughter, and I am loved!

JOURNALING PAGES

What does God being a good Father mean to you?

What do you love about your family? What's challenging about your family?

DAY 61

When You're Nervous About Jobs

I sought the LORD, and he answered me and rescued me from all my fears.—PSALM 34:4

What do you imagine doing for your job when you get older? Do you want to be a doctor or a teacher? An artist or a veterinarian? A computer programmer or an engineer? It is so fun to think about the future and even start practicing now!

Is the job you dream about something your mom or dad does? When I was growing up, my dad worked in real estate. I thought it was a fun adventure to ride around town, looking at all kinds of different houses, dreaming about which one I might buy one day.

Adults' jobs come and go, though, and they can change quickly. While this is totally normal, it can be scary for us when we don't know how it will affect us. We wonder, *Will we have to move? Will my parent(s) be unhappy? What if we don't have enough money until the next job?* Job changes can bring up a lot of questions and a lot of emotions.

Thankfully, their jobs aren't something you need to control. While their work affects you, it's one more thing you can trust God to handle. So when you hear conversations about new jobs, lost jobs, stressful jobs, or jobs in other towns, don't let that scare you.

God has a plan for your parents' or guardians' lives just as He has a plan for yours. He cares about their jobs and the work they do just as much He cares about what you do. He can be trusted with the jobs they have, the jobs they want, and the jobs they gain or lose. And one day, when you fill out your first job application, you can trust God with your job too!

Rest in that.

Thank You for reminding me, God, that You are always in control. That means You're in control of adults' jobs and lives too! I trust You.

When You Want All A's

Whatever you do, in word or in deed, do everything in the name of the Lord Jesus, giving thanks to God the Father through him.—COLOSSIANS 3:17

Do report-card days make you nervous? Sometimes it's exciting to see your grades, and sometimes you dread it. It all depends on what the report card says! Have you ever been surprised by what's there? Maybe you thought you were doing okay in a class, but the grade was lower than you expected. Or better yet, maybe it was the other way around!

Whatever the case, how much time do you spend thinking about your grades? Most of us want to do well in class and make our teachers and parents proud. But sometimes a subject in school is just plain tough, and the A's are hard to come by.

Here's the good news: God's not worried about how many A's you have. He's more concerned about your heart and mind.

Does this mean you don't have to study or do your schoolwork? Nope! But as you think about grades, look at today's Bible verse.

God gave you a sharp mind. Using that gift *for His glory* is what matters most. That means it's more important to be responsible with your time and talent than it is to get 100 on a test. It means if you need to study to learn the material, you spend the time doing the work and don't cheat or cut corners. Be responsible with that smart mind of yours!

Finally, don't take up all your mental energy worrying about your grades when you could use that energy to sit down and do the work instead. Study, read, listen, and learn. When we are responsible with our time and our minds, we can trust that God's never worried about the final grade.

Rest in that.

God, thank You for giving me the chance to use my mind! Would You help me not worry about grades but instead be faithful and responsible with the work I have in front of me?

DAY 63

When You Want People to Like You

Welcome one another, just as Christ also welcomed you, to the glory of God.—ROMANS 15:7

Do people like me? I've asked myself this question a lot. In fact, the number of times I've replayed a scene of meeting new friends in my head—mostly to try to figure out what they thought of me—is one too many.

Do you do that too? I hope your answer is no! I hope you feel confident in who God made you to be and you don't spend too much time wondering if everyone wants to be your friend. But I also know how we girls can be. We want the other girls to like our clothes, we want to make them laugh, and we want to be included.

What if I told you that worrying about what people think of you doesn't have to keep you up at night? I totally understand why we want everyone to like us, but not even Jesus was liked by everybody! If we let our minds spin and spin about being liked all the time, we'll never truly relax into who God made us to be.

The truth is we can spend time thinking about how everyone feels about us, or we can turn our thoughts around and think more about how we interact with and treat other people.

Be kind to everyone around you. Seek out those who seem lonely and left out. Forgive others quickly. Cheer on your friends in good times, and comfort them in hard times. This is how Jesus acted, and He can help us live this way too.

When you live the way Jesus did—leading with love, compassion, and concern for others—you will start to notice that people want to be around you. Do you know why? They see something different about you! And that difference is Jesus.

Rest in that.

God, will You help me love other people the way You love them? When I'm worried about whether people like me, will You remind me that my worth is found in You? Will You help me focus more on others and less on myself?

When You're Having a Bad Day

Our momentary light affliction is producing for us an absolutely incomparable eternal weight of glory. So we do not focus on what is seen, but on what is unseen. For what is seen is temporary, but what is unseen is eternal.
—2 CORINTHIANS 4:17–18

The Bible has a lot of stories of people having bad days, so when you have a day when it feels like nothing is going right, you're not alone. Have you heard some of these?

When Daniel was put in a lion's den (Daniel 6).

When Shadrach, Meshack, and Abednego were thrown in a fire (Daniel 3).

When Jonah got swallowed by a big fish (Jonah 1).

When Ruth's husband died and she was left poor (Ruth 1).

When Joseph's brothers sold him into slavery (Genesis 37).

When Esther learned Haman was planning to murder her people (Esther 3–4).

When Paul was thrown into prison (yet again) (Acts 23–24).

It was a bad day for each of these people in the Bible. Can you imagine any of these things happening to you? How scary, right? But do you know who comes through in every single one of those stories? God!

On your bad days, you may not face a giant, a lion, or a murderer, but you'll still face hard things. So when you fail a test, your parents don't understand you, or the boy you like keeps ignoring you, remember bad days don't stay bad forever. Remember the One who can turn the bad into something good.

The Bible is one big story of God showing up for His people. So on the good days and the bad days, we have a God who is right there with us—for all of it.

Rest in that.

God, bad days are not fun, and they make me sad, but thank You for being there even on the bad days! Would You help my heart heal, and would You bring joy for tomorrow?

DAY 65

When Everything Is Changing

Don't worry about anything, but in everything, through prayer and petition with thanksgiving, present your requests to God. And the peace of God, which surpasses all understanding, will guard your hearts and minds in Christ Jesus.—PHILIPPIANS 4:6–7

Think about the ocean for a second. Have you ever been swimming in the waves? Did you see any fish or seaweed?

When the waves started getting bigger—maybe even taller than you—were you tossed around without anything to hold onto? Did you try to plant your feet in one place, but the ground kept moving out from under you?

When everything starts changing in our lives, it can feel like we're being tossed around in the waves of life too—tall, strong, emotional waves.

Those waves could be because of a new school, new friends, a new town—or maybe it's not even such big things! Maybe small changes are adding up: You started playing soccer on a new team or joined a new class at church. Your brother is off to high school, so you won't see him in the hallway any-more. One of your parents took a new job, so you have more chores to do around the house. Whatever it may be, change can make you feel like everything around you is moving and you can't find your footing.

Did you know God cares about every part of that? When everything is changing, He's not upset to hear what you think about it. You can take every request, every prayer, and every worry to Him. He can be your steady ground. Ask Him to help you learn the names of the people in your new class. Ask Him to help you get through the school day without your brother. Tell Him when you're scared or excited or don't even know what to feel. He can calm the waves of your heart and mind today and tomorrow.

Rest in that.

God, I don't like when it feels like everything is changing, but I'm thankful You're always with me in it. Will You calm my mind and heart when I start to worry about it all?

When You're Worried About Your Family

I call to God, and the LORD will save me.—PSALM 55:16

My favorite movie as a kid was *The Lion King* (and in my day we only had the cartoon version). I could barely watch the scene where Mufasa dies, though. It broke my heart every single time (still does!).

Movies and TV shows are fun to watch, but sometimes they put scenarios in our heads that scare us into thinking the same thing will happen to us. When we see someone die during a movie, it not only makes us sad, but we start to think, *Is that about to happen to my family?*

Sometimes questions like this are just hypothetical, meaning they reflect an imaginary situation, but other times they are rooted in reality. Maybe one of your parents has a dangerous job or is battling an illness. Whatever the case, what-if scenarios can be overwhelming. And God can help you through every part of that.

A great first step is to think about what's *real*. If you're having a nightmare because you watched a scary movie (not real) or you've stressed yourself out over an idea (not real), ask God to help you stay present with what's going on here and now.

1. Pray: *God, show me what is true and real today.*

Secondly, if a family member is heading to do something that makes you nervous, take it to God. Ask Him to protect your mom, dad, brother, or sister.

2. Pray: *God, will You protect my _____ and keep them safe? Will You also calm my mind and give me peace?*

There is nothing you will face that God has not seen before, and there's nothing you will fear that He can't guide you through.

Rest in that.

God, thank You for being a Protector. Will You help calm my mind when I worry about my family and their safety? I know I can trust You to help me through it.

DAY 67

When It Feels Like Everyone Else Is Better than You

Now as we have many parts in one body, and all the parts do not have the same function, in the same way we who are many are one body in Christ and individually members of one another.—ROMANS 12:4–5

Do you ever see a video on TikTok or see a girl's post on Instagram and start wishing you had her hair? It's just the right color and falls in all the right places—and now you can't stand to look at yourself in a mirror.

Comparison can ruin just about anything. You think someone else's dress at the dance is cuter, so you're ashamed of what you're wearing. A classmate gets a better grade, so you've determined you are not smart. Your sister didn't get in trouble like you did, so you've decided you are not a good kid.

Comparison plants a lie in your head about who you are because you start seeing yourself as less than others. When you compare yourself to others, it's like you put on glasses that give you blurry vision. You can no longer see yourself (or anything) clearly because you are too worried about not being good enough or looking cute enough.

I want to help you fight the urge to compare yourself to other girls starting now because it will save you so much heartache for years to come. I want you to see yourself the way God sees you and live confidently in that—not bragging about yourself, but resting in the reality that God made you unique and special, unlike anyone else.

If every single person looked the same, wore the same thing, and acted the same way, we would never get to see the creativity of God. We couldn't celebrate diversity. God painted a beautiful masterpiece when He made you, and your colors stand out on their own! Take off the comparison glasses so you can see your true colors clearly.

Rest in that.

God, thank You for making me to be like no one else! Would You help me rest in that and celebrate instead of comparing myself to other girls? Would You help me celebrate my friends' uniqueness too?

When You Don't Know What to Pray

May the Lord of peace himself give you peace always in every way.—2 THESSALONIANS 3:16

Did you know that one of the many names for Jesus is "Prince of Peace"?

Isaiah 9:6 says, "For a child will be born for us, a son will be given to us, and the government will be on his shoulders. He will be named Wonderful Counselor, Mighty God, Eternal Father, Prince of Peace."

Because Jesus is always with us, we always have access to peace through Him. He is the reason we can find rest.

When you feel like you're having a hard time breathing because anxiety is taking over, when things around you are getting too loud and chaotic, or when it feels like you're getting tossed around . . . you can ask Jesus for peace!

Sometimes when I'm so overwhelmed that I don't know how to pray, I just say Jesus' name over and over again because His name alone is calming: "Jesus . . . Jesus . . . Jesus." I say it as I breathe in and out slowly—breathing in through my nose and out through my mouth, like I'm trying to blow out a candle. When we call His name, He hears us every time. Although you may not be able to clearly tell Him what's bothering you, He knows (Romans 8:26).

So the next time anxiety starts to steal your joy, remember that you know the Prince of Peace. He's not a cartoon character or a Disney movie prince or a made-up legend. He's Jesus—your God, your Creator, your Savior, your Friend.

Say His name! You're going to be okay.

Rest in that.

I'm taking a deep breath, Jesus, and trusting You. Would You give me peace as I rest tonight and as I wake up in the morning?

When You Have to Be Brave

"Be strong and courageous; don't be terrified or afraid of them. For the LORD your God is the one who will go with you; he will not leave you or abandon you."—DEUTERONOMY 31:6

Brave. It's a word I kind of like, but kind of don't want to like. Here's why: I think brave people are cool! I admire them. When tough things come their way, they seem to just take a deep breath and go for it.

But here's the thing. Looking brave and being brave are not the same. We all may appear to be brave when we make it through getting a shot without crying (and it's okay if you don't!), but the reality is you may be terrified on the inside.

Bravery comes from God. And so do you. The truth is, you're going to face some days when you need strength and you need bravery. Maybe there's a new zip line at camp and you need a little courage to jump off the edge! Or maybe you need a lot of bravery during a hospital stay, a funeral, or a big move. On the days when a lot of bravery is necessary, let me remind you of this: In any moment, big or small, when everything's too overwhelming or painful, you can rest.

When a doctor's office feels like the place where everything hurts . . .

When the needle pricks and pokes won't stop . . .

When you need someone to hold your hand . . .

You can be brave because God makes you brave.

When the moving truck is on the way . . .

When you're headed to camp and you don't know anyone else who will be there . . .

When you're listening to what will happen at the funeral . . .

You can be strong because God makes you strong.

He will give you what you need.

He will carry you through.

Rest in that.

Thank You, God, for helping me be brave on the broken days, the nervous days, and all the days in between.

When You're Dreading Something

When I am filled with cares, your comfort brings me joy.
—PSALM 94:19

I have a confession to make: I really don't like going to the dentist. I never wanted to admit that growing up because my aunt Helen was my dental hygienist and the dentist, Dr. Ted, was the friendliest man you'll ever meet. Still, I dreaded going every single time. I didn't like having my teeth cleaned or getting a filling. The only good part about it was getting to pick something fun from the treasure box at the end. I always went for the sugar-free gum . . . until I had braces!

Do you ever feel the dread of something creeping in the night before, the day before, even the week before the thing is scheduled to happen? I used to feel that way before going to the dentist. This feeling can turn our days upside down, and sometimes we don't even realize why. We carry the negative emotions around with us, not recognizing they don't have anything to do with what's happening today. Instead, they're connected to the things we're dreading in the future.

When this starts to happen, ask God to replace the feeling of really not wanting to do something with joy.

The truth is, the anticipation of going to the dentist was often worse than actually being there! As soon as I walked into the office, I'd see all the familiar faces, catch up with my aunt, and (despite the uncomfortable cleaning in the middle) be well on my way to a new toothbrush and treat from the treasure box. The dentist's office held some delight for me after all.

God can give you joy when you think it's not possible. He loves to do that! He's a God of comfort and light, and He can change your dread into delight.

Rest in that.

God, You are delightful. I'm dreading _____ right now. Would You take that away and help me find joy?

JOURNALING PAGES

What has scared you recently or made you really sad?

What verse could you memorize from this past week of devotions to help you remember God is protecting you? Write the verse out multiple times below to help you remember it.

When Your Feelings Are Hurt

Better an open reprimand than concealed love. The wounds of a friend are trustworthy, but the kisses of an enemy are excessive.—PROVERBS 27:5–6

You're not my friend anymore."

It makes my stomach turn upside down just thinking about these words. But I've heard them before, and maybe you have too.

Navigating fights with our friends can be hard, and we girls can be particularly mean to each other. I wish it weren't true, but we so often say things we don't mean. Or worse, we say them because we are dead set on hurting the person who hurt us.

Words don't simply get erased or deleted. They stay in our minds for a long time and leave us pushing replay, repeating them over and over again.

I can't step in and tell you why your friend said what she said, but I can tell you that you're loved no matter what.

So as you approach hard conversations with friends who have hurt you, do so with grace. Attempt to have a conversation about what's going on your friendship, and let each other share and listen. Many times, it's just a disagreement that you need to talk through, or your friend has been really hurt by something you didn't even know you did, and you need to hear her out.

When this is the case, you can ask God to guide you through the hard conversation. He's given us the Holy Spirit to live within us as our Counselor. He can nudge us when it's time to speak and when it's time to listen. He can help us admit when we are wrong. He can help heal and restore the relationship.

Ultimately, if a friendship ends, it will be sad for a while, but you will be okay. Friends will come and go, but God will remain by your side.

Rest in that.

Sometimes being a friend isn't easy, God. Would You continue to show me when to apologize and listen? Thank You for the friends I have! Would You help us treat each other with kindness and respect?

DAY 72

When You're Missing Your People

"I will be the same until your old age, and I will bear you up when you turn gray. I have made you, and I will carry you; I will bear and rescue you."—ISAIAH 46:4

Today's topic was supposed to be about when *you* get homesick and miss your friends and family. But you know what? As I'm writing this, I'm sitting in a cabin that some generous friends let me borrow for the weekend, and *I'm* the one who's homesick. Yep, me! An adult who thought going away alone to write would be fun (and don't get me wrong, it is!) but quickly realized it was lonely too.

It's okay to miss your people. And when I say, "your people," I mean those you're closest to: your family and your friends. You love your people dearly! They're important to you. For example, have you ever gone to a sleepover or an overnight camp and things felt unfamiliar and uncomfortable because your mom and dad weren't there to say goodnight? Or your best friend wasn't right next to you? This feeling is normal.

So when your heart is sad because you're longing to be with your family or friends, try praying these three things. (And I'm going to do the same in my cabin!)

1. Thank God for your people. Mention them by name.

2. Ask God to give you peace where you are while you're away from them.

3. Ask God to help you love those around you (and even make new friends).

Finally, rest in the fact that just as God can be with you at all times, He can be with your family and friends too. You're okay with Him, and so are they.

Rest in that.

Thank You, God, for my friends and family and for always being with me and them, even when we are apart.

DAY 73

When You Can't Fall Asleep

Those who trust in the LORD will renew their strength; they will soar on wings like eagles; they will run and not become weary, they will walk and not faint.—ISAIAH 40:31

Does sugar ever make you super hyper or so wired that you don't feel tired? What about caffeine? After any birthday party that includes cake, candy, or a soda, I am destined to be awake for a long time.

It's frustrating when you can't fall asleep when you want to, isn't it? I know people say to count sheep in your head, but does that actually work? What I see happening in my head is more of a Ferris wheel situation. I get on the ride, and it just keeps turning round . . . and round . . . and round . . . and I never get off.

At first I'm just frustrated I can't go to sleep. Then worry starts creeping in that if I never fall asleep, I won't be able to stay awake tomorrow. Have you been there?

The thing is—the faster we can calm our minds, the better. When our worry starts running away with tomorrow's plans and what-ifs, we end up sitting on that never-ending Ferris wheel instead of hopping off and finally falling asleep.

When I can't sleep, I talk to God. It calms me no matter what. I spent a lot of years feeling terrible if I accidently fell asleep while praying to Him, but one day I finally realized He considers it a joy for me to talk to Him *and* rest in Him.

You know the God who gives you strength. Talk to Him at night and trust Him to carry you through the day, no matter how much energy you have.

Rest in that.

God, I love that I can talk to You anytime, anywhere. Thank You for helping me calm down and rest!

DAY 74

When You Are Disappointed

Humble yourselves, therefore, under the mighty hand of God, so that he may exalt you at the proper time, casting all your cares on him, because he cares about you.—1 PETER 5:6–7

Your parents said no to you going to a friend's birthday party this weekend.

You didn't get the part you wanted in the play.

Your cast isn't coming off in time to try out for the soccer team.

None of your friends are in your new class.

Different things disappoint us all the time. We have an idea of how we want things to go—how we see our weekend playing out, or how we want our outfit to look—and when reality doesn't live up to the expectation, we feel all kinds of emotions. We might be mad or annoyed or sad. And whether the disappointment is over a big thing or a small thing, it can really mess with our day and our mind.

God cares about your disappointments. He cares when you're sad your friend went to another birthday party instead of yours. He cares when you're frustrated your dad couldn't be at your play. He cares when you're upset the movie you wanted to see is sold out. And He cares when you're disappointed with Him too.

Your feelings matter to God. They're not a burden on Him.

First Peter 5:7 reminds us, "[Cast] all your cares on him, because he cares about you." You don't have to keep all your disappointments to yourself. God is big enough and strong enough to hold them for you—and He wants to.

Rest in that.

God, thank You for seeing me when I'm disappointed. Thank You for caring! Will You bring peace to my heart when I feel disappointed?

When You're Having Friends Over

The LORD will be your confidence and will keep your foot from a snare.—PROVERBS 3:26

Do you ever have friends over for play dates? What about for a sleepover or a party? When you're waiting for them to come over, how do you feel? Excited? Nervous? Eager for them to arrive?

Inviting friends to your house is super fun, and it's one of the easiest ways to ways to get to know each other better! Your friends get to see you in your element—they get to see your room, your family, your clothes, and your toys.

All this can be fun to share with them . . . unless it's not. What if your little brother ends up being really annoying? What if they don't have as much fun at your house as you hoped? What if there's something you're embarrassed for them to see?

This may seem silly, but my family used to have several old clown paintings that my mom hung in the hallway leading up to my room. When friends came over, I hoped and prayed they didn't see the clown pictures, because nine times out of ten, people thought they were creepy.

Is there anything you worry your friends will notice and judge you for?

Whether you're worried about your equivalent of my clown paintings, or you're worried about not having the right snacks (because Cassidy's house always does!), remember that being yourself is exactly what your friends need to see. Proverbs 3:26 reminds us, "The Lord will be your confidence." What's most important is that your friends see God through you when you spend time together. The rest of it won't matter.

Rest in that.

God, would You help me to be confident and to show my friends how good You are? Would You help me worry less about being judged and more about loving people well?

When Your Nerves Are Getting to You

Protect me, God, for I take refuge in you.—Psalm 16:1

Having to give a speech or presentation in front of your class.

Singing a solo.

Taking a standardized test.

Getting ready for your first game.

Going to the doctor.

There are so many things that can make us nervous, and honestly, reading through that list makes my stomach jump! Do any of these events make you anxious? What's not on this list that makes your stomach turn?

Being in the spotlight, preparing to do something new, or putting all your preparation into one big day can make anybody—even the most daring among us—a little sweaty and anxious.

What I love about God is that He can bring a steadiness to a shaky-feeling day. When your voice is trembling as you start to give your speech, or you're short of breath when you step onto the field, find your safe place in God. Often the biggest source of our nerves is because we feel alone in whatever we're doing.

Remember: You're not the first one God has helped do this. Countless people have sung solos, played in big matches, and taken hard tests. Countless people have asked God for help. It may be your first time, but it's certainly not God's. You are experiencing what all of humanity has experienced in one way or another, and God is big enough to help all of us!

A little bit of nervousness won't hurt us, but when it keeps you from sleeping at night, focusing during the day, or feeling well overall, it needs to be shut down. God is bigger than your nerves and fear; He can protect you. No matter how the test, game, or presentation turns out, He is more than capable of carrying you through.

Rest in that.

Thank You for being my safe place, God, and for helping me be calm when I'm so nervous!

When You Need to Laugh

A joyful heart is good medicine, but a broken spirit dries up the bones.—PROVERBS 17:22

Have you ever heard someone laughing and giggling for so long that you start laughing too? You don't even know how it started, but now you're full-on belly laughing, tears starting to form in your eyes. It's the best feeling, right? You laugh so hard your stomach hurts!

When we get all worked up and worried about something, things can get too serious, and we just need to laugh a little to relieve the stress. In fact, the Bible tells us that a joyful heart is good medicine. That's a type of medicine I want! Don't you?

Think about this too: if someone else is having a really hard day, what could you do to help them smile or laugh? If your friend is nervous about a doctor's appointment or an upcoming performance, you can help bring a smile to their face with a joke or funny story. You can help relieve the stress and worry.

Sometimes going outside to play allows the fresh air to bring a wave of light over you too. Run through the sprinklers. Go find a swing. Climb a tree. Do something fun!

Laughing calms our minds and brings joy to our hearts. It puts smiles on our faces and other people's too. It may seem like the oddest thing to do when life is really serious. But that break from all the heavy things can remind you that joy exists and life won't always be this tough. Such hope comes from God, and it's what you need.

Rest in that.

Thank You for the gift of laughter, God! Thank You that the simplest things can make me smile. Would You help me find those moments of joy and laughter when things get hard?

When You Need to Find Things to Appreciate

Rejoice always, pray constantly, give thanks in everything; for this is God's will for you in Christ Jesus. —1 Thessalonians 5:16–18

One of my favorite things to do when it's someone's birthday is ask them what they were grateful for about the past year. It helps everyone stop for a moment and think about what we loved about the year before we start talking about hopes and dreams for the future.

Focusing on what we're thankful for isn't something we just do on Thanksgiving or at a birthday celebration. It can be a daily habit.

There are two benefits to frequently thanking God for the people and things He's given us: It reminds us that ultimately, everything belongs to Him. And it changes our mindset and attitude for the day. Gratitude can literally transform us.

So when you're having a day that's full of worry or difficulty, what if you stopped for a minute and named (even out loud) a few things you're thankful for? Would that change your attitude? Would that make you a more enjoyable person to be around?

To start making gratitude a daily habit, here are three questions to ask yourself:

1. What's something you love about God?

2. What's something you love in the world He made?

3. Who in your life could you thank God for?

What if you talked about these things with your family over dinner? Or before you go to sleep at night? How might it change your outlook and remind you of God's goodness?

We need to tell God what we love about Him and why we're grateful for what He's given us. It reminds us that He is the Creator, and we are the created. It reminds us that all of life is a gift.

Rest in that.

God, You are good! I am so thankful for You and for Your gift of _____. Thank You for loving me.

DAY 79

When You Think God's Going to Give Up

In him you also were sealed with the promised Holy Spirit when you heard the word of truth, the gospel of your salvation, and when you believed.—EPHESIANS 1:13

Have you ever tried to get your mom's attention while you're in a grocery store, but no matter what name you called her, she was so focused on finding the perfect bananas that she didn't hear you? *"Mom! Mama! Kathy! Hey!"* Eventually, you probably just gave up and waited for her to realize that even though she was pushing the cart toward the cereal aisle, you had already thrown your favorite (the ones with the marshmallows) in.

As funny as that can be, I think we sometimes can feel this way about calling out to God. *Is He there? Did He hear me?*

Maybe you are afraid you have forgotten about God one too many times, so He's going to forget about you. Or you're scared you have messed up one too many times, and He is staying mad at you. Maybe you still have a lot of questions about Him and you're worried that's going to annoy Him.

Humans have a limit to what we can handle, so we often think God does too. But He doesn't have a limit. God will always recognize your voice and not give up on you. The Bible shows us one example after another of people who continually let God down, yet He never turned away from them:

• When Abraham messed up again and again, God didn't give up on him. He built a nation through Abraham's family.

• When Moses messed up again and again, God didn't give up on him. He used Moses to help lead His people to freedom.

• When David messed up again and again, God didn't give up on him. In fact, it was through David's family line that Jesus was born.

God is faithful and true to His Word. He will hear your prayers and keep showing up for you.

Rest in that.

God, it is such a relief to know You'll never give up on me. Thank You for always listening to me, loving me, and showing up for me.

DAY 80

When You Like a Boy

*In him we have boldness and confident access through faith in him.—*Ephesians 3:12

Let's talk about boys, shall we?

This is the part where you're probably giggling or blushing or thinking boys are just gross. I get it! Crushes can be fun, they can be nerve-wracking, and they can take up a lot of your mental energy if you're not careful. When a crush becomes so distracting that it keeps you awake at night, you know it's time to consider if you're being wise with your heart, mind, and schedule.

There's nothing wrong with having a crush! But the way it impacts how you see yourself and how you judge your own worth is important. When you start wondering what a guy thinks about you, make sure you first know what God thinks about you. (Read Psalm 139 to start.) Who God says you are will always trump what a boy says you are.

Also, when all you can think about is how to get a boy's attention, take a step back and ask why. If you mostly want to know you matter, remember that God cherishes you. You matter more to Him than you will to any human.

When a boy starts to have a crush on you, show him kindness. Show him Jesus. Be yourself. Trust that God didn't make a mistake when He made you. Your confidence in who God made you is what your friends, and your crushes, will be drawn to.

Finally, don't rush any of this! It's wiser to wait to date until you're older; when the dating days begin, remember that God has a plan for all your relationships. Ask Him to remind you that you are loved when the dates come and when they don't—that your beauty comes from Him and not from attention from boys.

Remember you are loved, you are beautiful, and you are not alone.

Rest in that.

God, thank You for loving me! Thank You for reminding me that I'm loved. Will You help me remember this every day?

Do you ever worry about what other people think of you? Does it make you shy away from being yourself or making mistakes? Where do you get your confidence from right now? Where do you think it should come from?

Based on what you've read so far, write down some of the things God says and thinks about you. Why does this matter more than anything?

When the Next Step Is Hard

The LORD my Lord is my strength; he makes my feet like those of a deer and enables me to walk on mountain heights!
—Habakkuk 3:19

Have you ever seen a deer? I often see them at one of my favorite places to walk in Nashville—Radnor Lake. When I head into the wooded hills surrounding the lake, I typically spot them hanging out a little way off the trail, keeping watch on who's walking by while they enjoy a forest snack.

While the hills around Radnor Lake aren't too high, it doesn't matter to the deer. Small hills or big mountains, they can stand up without stumbling. They're sure-footed. Isn't that cool? If you or I were standing on the side of tall mountain, we'd have to hold on to something or hunch over to make sure we wouldn't fall. But not deer. They can stand up easily, and they can stay steady.

I know there are days when you feel like you're struggling to stand up because you're not sure what to do. Maybe you're torn over a big decision. Maybe you know you need to speak up about something but lack the courage. Maybe you need to end a friendship that isn't good for you. Whatever is bothering you, remember today's verse.

God makes you strong. He can give you steady feet like a deer and help you walk easily up whatever mountain you're trying to climb.

So when you don't know what to do, turn to God. There is nothing too big or too scary for Him. He can give you the strength, wisdom, and sure-footedness you need to take a tough step forward.

He's just that good.

Rest in that.

God, the fact that a deer can stand steadily on the mountainside is so cool! Thank You for giving me what I need when I'm not sure what step to take. Will You help me always remember that You can make me strong?

When You're Scared to Ask God

If any of you lacks wisdom, he should ask God—who gives to all generously and ungrudgingly—and it will be given to him. But let him ask in faith without doubting. For the doubter is like the surging sea, driven and tossed by the wind.—JAMES 1:5–6

When my friend was a kid, she used to have a "question quota" from her parents. This meant she was allowed to ask a certain number of questions a day. She loved to talk (still does!) and has always been curious, but she had so many questions that her parents gave her a limit!

I think we often approach God with this same mindset—that our questions or doubts or opinions might be too much for Him and there is a limit to what we can ask. So we stop ourselves from going to God, which increases our anxiety all the more!

But we read about person after person in the Bible asking God questions or asking Jesus questions while He was on earth. They wanted to know how to live. They wanted to know when they would receive what they were promised.

They wanted to know if Jesus could heal them. Plenty of the questions people asked in the Bible are the same ones we still ask today.

And you know what? God never turned His back on His people or cut off their questions. You can ask God anything. He's not afraid of your questions or your feelings. He doesn't have a question quota.

Waiting for answers requires patience, though. God may not answer the way you want Him to, or He may take a long time to answer. Be listening! As you pray, give Him a chance to respond. Open your Bible. God often speaks to us to through the words He's already given us there. He welcomes our curiosity with open arms.

Rest in that.

God, thank You for always letting me be me. It's comforting to know I can bring anything to You!

When Your Small Mistake Has a Big Impact

All have sinned and fall short of the glory of God; they are justified freely by his grace through the redemption that is in Christ Jesus.—ROMANS 3:23–24

I will never forget my eighth-grade chorus performance. We were doing a special tribute to all the eighth graders who were moving on to high school. During the song, each of us was supposed to take the microphone, say our names, and declare what high school we'd be going to. It all had to be right on time, though, or it would throw off the whole thing.

So guess what I did when it was my turn? Froze.

I don't remember why, but I do remember the look on my chorus director's face. Shock. Anger. We had practiced this moment so many times! It was supposed to be so simple. And I messed the whole thing up.

Have you ever had one of these moments? You missed a goal during your soccer game from a spot on the field you'd practiced over and over, or you forgot to do the chores your mom asked you to do even after you put a reminder on your door.

Listen: Mistakes happen. Bad grades happen. Losing a game happens.

It's okay to be sad or frustrated for a little bit, but don't stay that way too long. Don't start believing the lies that you can never score a goal, ace a test, or remember the words to a song.

God understands mistakes. He understands that the world is broken and no one is perfect. If we were perfect, we would have never needed a Savior to come save us. But we're people who make a lot of mistakes, and we still need Jesus every day. So the next time you make a mistake, remember that this is what it means to be human, and thank God that you don't have to be perfect because Jesus already is.

Rest in that.

God, I don't like to mess up, but thank You for reminding me that You know all humans will make mistakes. And thank You for sending Jesus to us. He's the only perfect Person ever!

When Your Body Is Changing

Don't you know that your body is a temple of the Holy Spirit who is in you, whom you have from God? You are not your own, for you were bought at a price. So glorify God with your body.—1 CORINTHIANS 6:19–20

Being a girl is so much fun! We do all kinds of things with our hair, try different styles of clothes, and paint our nails (if we want to). Having many options and choosing our style is fun!

But we girls also have plenty of things to figure out about our bodies, which can be fun and challenging at the same time. At your age, it might always feel like your body is changing or you're having to learn something new about taking care of it. And that's okay! Your body is an intricate instrument. Just like you may have learned how to take care of a clarinet when you joined band, you have to learn how to take care of your body now.

If you're worried about anything happening to your body as you grow and get older, know that God created your body to do this. It's not a mystery to Him, and it's not a mystery to your mom or sisters or other women around you who can help you through all the changes.

The Bible tells us our bodies are also temples—meaning they're holy places where God lives. Because of this, we care about how we treat our bodies. Your body's ever-changing size and shape doesn't have to be a scary discovery. Rest in the fact that God designed your body to do exactly what it should, and He has given you the resources to take care of it.

The God who made seasons to change, seeds to become trees, and caterpillars to transform into butterflies made your body to change too.

Rest in that.

God, all these things I have to learn about taking care of myself can be a little overwhelming, but I want to treat my body right because You gave it to me. Will You help me along the way?

DAY 85

When You Need to Calm Your Mind Before Bed

Finally brothers and sisters, whatever is true, whatever is honorable, whatever is just, whatever is pure, whatever is lovely, whatever is commendable—if there is any moral excellence and if there is anything praiseworthy—dwell on these things.—PHILIPPIANS 4:8

I know some days end in a sad place, and sometimes it doesn't hit you until you climb into your bed. You pull back the covers, grab your favorite stuffed animal (mine was a bunny), take a deep breath . . . and then the tears start flowing.

The day was hard, the day was scary, or the day was too busy. Whatever it may be, your mind is spinning again, and now the tears are flowing even harder.

In the book of Philippians, Paul reminded the people of Philippi to dwell on things that were true and honorable, lovely and commendable. Paul knew all too well that the things we set our minds on are what our hearts beat to as well.

He understood that this world is a rough place, but there is *always* something good to focus our attention on.

So, what if today, you think through some of those true, honorable, lovely, and commendable things to help settle your mind? Whether it's been a bad day or a great one, spending a few minutes answering these questions may be the thing you need to slow the spinning in your mind.

(Answer these questions out loud or write them down.)

1. What is one thing you are grateful for today?

2. What used to make your heart happy that you've forgotten about recently?

3. What is one true thing about God that you need to focus on?

God is good even when we have hard days, and He can help you remember the good when it feels like everything is too much.

Rest in that.

God, will You help me settle my mind and focus on what is good and true? I am so thankful for You!

When You Think God Is Going to Change His Mind About You

Today the LORD has affirmed that you are his own possession as he promised you, that you are to keep all his commands, that he will elevate you to praise, fame, and glory above all the nations he has made, and that you will be a holy people to the LORD your God as he promised.—DEUTERONOMY 26:18–19

When you're at a restaurant, staring at a menu, is it easy for you to decide what to order? Growing up, I had one thing I'd almost always choose off the menu: chicken fingers. Choosing wasn't hard for me then, but now that I'm older and have widened my food horizon, making a decision can be a challenge. I place my order with the waiter but then hear what my friend orders and want to change my mind. Does that ever happen to you?

We humans are fickle. We go back and forth all the time—on little things and big things. For example, even Jesus' closest friends couldn't fully decide about following Him. Three different times, Jesus' disciple Peter denied knowing Him to protect himself. Three times! Jesus even predicted this would happen, and it sounded like a crazy idea, but it turned out to be true.

But guess what? Jesus never changed His mind about Peter. Jesus continued to love him and serve him—all the way up to when He died on the cross for Peter's (and our) sins.

Do you ever wonder if God will change His mind about you? As a fickle human being, you will mess up. You might doubt God or deny Him. You might get mad at Him or ignore Him, but He won't ever turn His back on you. So don't let your sins or frustrations make you pull away from God. In fact, He wants you to bring all of it to Him. He wants it so badly, He sent Jesus to live on earth and die in our place, so we could have eternal life with Him.

You can stop worrying that God will walk away from you, because He is not capable of it.

Rest in that.

God, thank You that I can rest without worrying if you'll change Your mind about me!

When You're Worried People Don't Like You

LORD, you have searched me and known me.—PSALM 139:1

Making new friends can often be hard. It's hard to find a good friend, and it's hard to be one! When it comes to friendship, it's always a good idea to think about how you're treating other people: Are you being kind? Are you listening well? Are you treating others like you would want to be treated? Even if your answer is "Yes!" every time, you still might not click with everyone.

Do you ever start down these rabbit trails?

Because this one person doesn't like me, no one will like me.

Because a few people don't understand me, no one understands me.

When I look in the mirror, I don't look like the prettiest girl I know—I'm not pretty at all.

None of this is true!

The Bible tells us what's true about ourselves even when we're not sure. If you're wondering if what you think is what God thinks, open your Bible. Ask for help finding verses that talk about what God thinks about you, like today's verse in Psalm 139:1.

Then take what you think and see if it matches with what the Bible says. If it matches, it's true! If it doesn't match, it's a lie. Let's try a few:

- **I'm thinking:** *No one cares what I think.*

- The Bible says: "Don't let anyone despise your youth, but set an example for the believers" (1 Timothy 4:12).

- **I'm thinking:** *No one is ever going to like me.*

- The Bible says: "Am I now trying to persuade people, or God? Or am I striving to please people? If I were still trying to please people, I would not be a servant of Christ" (Galatians 1:10).

When you question who you are or what matters, go to the Bible. There you'll find what's true.

Rest in that.

Thank You for reminding me of who You say I am. Will You help me be confident as I make new friends and find friends who are kind?

When You Need to Stand Up for What You Believe

"Love the Lord your God with all your heart, with all your soul, with all your mind, and with all your strength. The second is, Love your neighbor as yourself. There is no other command greater than these."—MARK 12:30–31

Have you ever been picked on for standing up for something you believed in? It doesn't feel very good, does it? It makes you feel all alone and might even make you question the thing you're standing up for.

Let's talk about Noah and the ark for a minute. Have you ever heard that story from Genesis 7? If you have, you probably learned about how Noah built this giant boat and then gathered two of each animal on the earth, along with his family, and secured everyone on board before the whole world flooded. Noah saved the day, because everything and everyone left behind was swept away by the water.

But think about all the days leading up to the flood. God had given Noah specific information about the size of the ark and why He would send a flood. Noah did everything God asked Him to do, and while we don't know what the other people were thinking at the time, we can imagine they were curious why this six-hundred-year-old man was building a giant boat. They must have thought he was crazy!

God has also asked us to sometimes do unpopular things. While God hasn't commanded us to build a gigantic boat, He has asked us to love Him with everything we are, and to love our neighbors as ourselves. These are the main instructions for our lives. Will we obey them without caring what other people think? Noah's obedience helped save humanity. Who in your life might get to meet God because of your obedience to Him?

You can stand up for what you believe in and not worry about what others think because you are part of a bigger story: God's story.

Rest in that.

God, would You help me stand strong in following You when it feels like no one else is? And would You help me love others too so they can know You?

DAY 89

When You Don't Want to Get Sick

Heal me, LORD, and I will be healed; save me, and I will be saved, for you are my praise.—JEREMIAH 17:14

No one likes being sick. Even if a head cold means getting to watch a little extra TV, the sneezing and coughing and runny nose are enough to make you miserable pretty quickly. And don't get me started about throwing up. It's the worst, right? I will fight as long as I can to not throw up, because I can't think of anything more miserable.

Do you ever worry about getting sick? Maybe someone you've been around has been sick, and you're afraid you will catch whatever they had. Or maybe you're scared you will catch something while at school and be too sick to attend an upcoming birthday party.

Sometimes we can get so worked up about the idea of getting sick that we start to feel it in our bodies. Our stomachs twist because we're nervous, or our heads throb because we're stressed.

When this happens to you, tell God how you're feeling and how you don't want to get sick. Ask Him for protection and good health. He hears you, and you can trust Him with your body.

God is a protector, but He's also a healer. If you do get sick, ask Him to heal you. He's healed people who have been sick for years, He has given vision back to those who were blind, and He's allowed people to walk who never could. God can do all things! But even if He doesn't, He is still good. He is still with you.

Rest in that.

God, would You protect me and my family from getting sick? Would You also help me from worrying about it? I trust that You will protect me!

When You Think About Heaven

As it is written, "What no eye has seen, no ear has heard, and no human heart has conceived—God has prepared these things for those who love him."—1 CORINTHIANS 2:9

Do you ever think about heaven? You probably haven't had to think about it unless someone you know has passed away. Usually those moments are so sad because you miss the person, but if they're in heaven, it's comforting to remember they are with God!

I think about heaven sometimes. I think about the people I'll see, what it will be like to worship God, and what everything will look like. Because I've never seen heaven, though, it often leaves me with more and more questions. Do you feel that way? Maybe the idea of heaven even makes you a little nervous because it seems like a big mystery.

The Bible gives us a sneak peek of what's to come, though. It says:

• God will make all things new—there will be a new heaven and a new earth. (Revelation 21:1)

- We will have new bodies. (Philippians 3:21)

- There will be no death, no sadness, and no pain. (Revelation 21:4)

Can you imagine how incredible heaven will be? Your brothers and sisters in Christ will be there, all that is hard and broken will be restored, and we will get to worship God forever. We will never get bored because we will be with our limitless God, who will make everything perfect again. Forever.

Think on these things the next time the thought of heaven makes you anxious. God's given us the Bible to help us understand what eternity with Him will be like. And when I read all these reminders of what's to come, I can't wait!

God has prepared an amazing, better-than-you-can-imagine, place for you.

Rest in that.

God, I love what I read about heaven! Thank You for giving me that to look forward to and for promising to restore everything!

JOURNALING PAGES

What things in your life are changing right now? Is change hard for you, or is it exciting?

What do you want to ask God for this week? Is there anything you're afraid to ask Him? Tell Him what's on your mind. Tell Him what you need.

When You Feel Like You Don't Matter

It was you who created my inward parts; you knit me together in my mother's womb. I will praise you because I have been remarkably and wondrously made. Your works are wondrous, and I know this very well.—PSALM 139:13–14

Has anyone ever made you feel like you didn't matter? People's words can cut deep, whether they mean to or not. Someone in high school once told me I didn't have a personality, and that statement stuck with me for years. It wasn't until I was an adult that I realized how much I had believed it about myself.

As girls, we can spend far too much time worrying about something mean someone has said to us or about us. We can take those words and, in turn, be really hard on ourselves. This is the opposite of what God wants for us.

Your feelings are valid! Mean words rip through us, and it's hard to forget them. But they don't have the final say regarding who you are. God didn't forget anything when He made you. He didn't skip a step when creating your personality or forget to count the number of hairs on your head when designing your skin tone and hair texture (Luke 12:7). You might not understand (or even like) why God made you how He did, but it's important to remember God made you on purpose and with a purpose.

There is no one else on this earth like you, and in case you needed a reminder, that's a beautiful thing. You were made in God's image, which means you get to reflect some of what He's like—you're like a mirror shining a picture of God to the people around you. How cool is that?

So the next time other people's mean words are ringing in your ears, open your Bible to Psalm 139. Read the whole thing. Ask God to show you why He made you, and remember that what God makes is special. Every single time.

Rest in that.

God, thank You for reminding me I'm special and You didn't mess up when You made me. I love what You create! When other people's words hurt, will You remind me that I'm loved (and created!) by You?

When You Can't Stop Thinking About Something

Let your eyes look forward; fix your gaze straight ahead.
—PROVERBS 4:25

Have you ever created a countdown for something you were excited about? Maybe it was a trip to Disney World or your first visit to an overnight camp. Did you keep track of the number of days left and create a to-do list for every little thing leading up to it? Did you daydream about the outfits you would wear and the activities you would do? Did you even start dreading the moment it would all be over?

You will always know I'm excited about an upcoming trip because I start typing out a list in the Notes app on my phone. I look up things to do in the city I'll be visiting, add it to my list, and then start documenting everything I need to pack!

The anticipation of something fun on the horizon is thrilling (and sometimes distracting). There is absolutely nothing wrong with being excited about something, but if the dreaming and planning are getting in the way of focusing on what's going on right now, that's a problem.

When this happens to you, I suggest pulling out a journal to help. Give yourself a few minutes a day to write down what you're excited about and what you're thinking about. It's like your little window in the day to celebrate! Then, when you're done, close the journal and put it away. Use that as a visual reminder to focus on what's in front of you right now.

Sometimes we are restless because we're so excited about what's to come that we miss what God is doing in the present. As you journal, ask Him to help you feel that same kind of hopeful joy you have about an upcoming trip on your normal, everyday, run-of-the-mill days too. Your excited heart brings God joy, and He can give you that delight in life every single day.

Rest in that.

I love having things to look forward to, God! Thank You for those feelings. When I am so distracted by them, though, will You help me be present and find joy in the day You've given me?

When It's Not What You Had Planned

We know that all things work together for the good of those who love God, who are called according to his purpose.
—Romans 8:28

When COVD-19 hit in 2020 and schools started closing (then eventually went to virtual learning), I felt so bad for all of you. I knew none of you imagined your school year going that way. You expected to see your friends every day, talk to your teacher in person, and still have normal class parties and plays and sports. You had to get creative in staying connected to classmates, and you had to adjust your schedules and routines to fit the new plan you didn't ask for. How was that experience for you?

There will always be things that don't go according to our plans. The impact might not be as big as that of a global pandemic, but we will still have days we don't expect.

For example, when you think back on 2020, I bet you can remember some things you were grateful for, right? Maybe it was going on lots of family walks or being able to wear pajamas while you did your schoolwork. Maybe it was having more time to learn a new skill or video chat more with relatives who lived far away.

When life doesn't go the way we planned, pointing out the good things can help shift our hearts and minds. It can help us fight the fears of what's coming next and focus on what we know to be true.

God has a plan. Always. And when things aren't the way we imagined, we can start to worry that nothing will ever go right again. Fight against that lie. Look for the good things right in front of you. Thank God for them, and trust that yesterday, today, and tomorrow, He's working everything together for good.

Rest in that.

God, will You help me recognize things I'm thankful for when things don't go as planned? Would You help me trust that You have a good plan even when I can't see it?

When Both Ideas Are Good

Whether you eat or drink, or whatever you do, do everything for the glory of God.—1 CORINTHIANS 10:31

Do you love all the things that summer vacation brings? If you get the summer off from school, it might mean camps and pools and riding bikes and time with friends. And it's just the best! Summer is a chance to try new things, stay up a little later, be outside as much as possible, and give your mind a break from schoolwork.

But do you ever have a hard time choosing what to do because two ideas sound so great?

Maybe you're trying to decide between spending a week at your grandmother's house (you love baking with her) or going to basketball camp (your best friend is going). Or maybe you can't decide one day whether to go to the pool or work on a craft at home. We humans hate that we can't be in two places at once! But eventually we have to decide.

Making decisions, big or small, doesn't always mean one idea is better than the other. Instead, *you get to choose*. We often talk to God about the big (hard) decisions in our lives, but we forget He can help us with the small (fun) ones too. God cares about things like where you go to school and what sport you play, but He also cares about your daily life choices. He cares about your pool day and your art class, your day at home with your siblings and your camping trip.

Ask God for direction, and then use the mind He gave you to make a decision! Once you do, trust that God is faithful no matter what you decided.

Rest in that.

God, thank You for good things, even when I have to decide between them! Will You help me in the big decisions and the small ones? Will You help me be content with the decision I've made?

DAY 95

When You Regret Something

Brothers and sisters, I do not consider myself to have taken hold of it. But one thing I do: Forgetting what is behind and reaching forward to what is ahead, I pursue as my goal the prize promised by God's heavenly call in Christ Jesus.
—PHILIPPIANS 3:13–14

Have you ever had trouble sleeping because you regretted something you did that day?

There have been many nights when I've lain in bed replaying conversations in my head, trying to figure out why I said or did something I shouldn't have. But it may not be something like that for you! Maybe you decided not to go on a trip with your friend's family because you were nervous to be gone from home that long, and now you regret not going. Or perhaps you had to decide between playing volleyball and doing the school play, and you wish you could change your decision.

How do you handle regret?

It can be easy to let our minds go back over the thing we're missing out on or the thing we wish we had done. This pattern might lead us to feeling guilty about what we've done or feeling bad about ourselves. When you begin to replay those moments that fill you with regret, ask God to help you move forward and move past it.

Letting our minds run away with the things we wish we had done differently will only leave us thinking about the past all the time. As today's verse reminds us, we can forget what is behind and reach forward to what is ahead. Why? Because God makes everything new, every single day (Lamentations 3:22–23).

God will help you overcome the regret.

Rest in that.

God, thank You for helping me get past the things I regret! I love that every day is a new day because of You. Will You help me remember this truth each morning?

DAY 96

When You Are Weary

"Come to me, all of you who are weary and burdened, and I will give you rest. Take up my yoke and learn from me, because I am lowly and humble in heart, and you will find rest for your souls. For my yoke is easy and my burden is light."
—MATTHEW 11:28–30

I think there's a reason *weary* rhymes with *teary*.

When our bodies and minds are both tired, we often find ourselves in tears. Sometimes we don't even know why the tears are flowing, but when we stop for a second we realize just how exhausted we are. We're weary from all the changes going on around us and inside us. We're weary from broken hearts. Even an annoying sibling can make us weary!

Bring your weariness—your tears, your aching shoulders, your heavy eyes—to Jesus. Sit still with Him. Rest. Pick up your Bible. Turn on worship music.

In today's verses, Jesus reminds us that He is gentle. When everything feels too heavy, we need His gentle, calming care to give us rest. And Jesus isn't just talking about sleep. He says, *rest for our souls*. Jesus restores us from the inside out.

Jesus understands a weary world, because He came to live on earth in order to redeem it. So, when *tired* and *exhausted* are the only words that describe how you're feeling, don't just tell your mom, dad, or best friend. Tell God.

Take a deep breath and exhale a sigh of relief because Jesus can carry all the heavy things weighing you down. You can lean on His steady shoulder. You can rest.

Jesus is our peace, and as the Christmas song "O Holy Night" reminds us, He brings "a thrill of hope. The weary world rejoices."

Rest in that.

Jesus, I can take a deep breath because I know I can find rest in You. Will You carry this weight and heaviness I feel? Thank You for giving me hope and peace.

When You Feel Stuck in a Hard Place

We also rejoice in our afflictions, because we know that affliction produces endurance, endurance produces proven character, and proven character produces hope.—ROMANS 5:3–4

Have you ever been sick for more than two days, and you find yourself counting down the minutes until you can get back to normal? You start missing school, aching for your friends, and you just want your body to feel better again!

Maybe you were quarantined during the crazy days of the COVID-19 pandemic. Whether you were sick or were just exposed to the virus, you needed to stay home for a long time, and the days started all feeling the exact same. *Will it ever end?* you wondered.

This question can creep in when anything gets hard or exhausting. *How long? Is it over yet? Will this last forever?* While you may not have an answer to any of those questions, you do have a God who is with you when it's hard, and He can use these hard moments to help you grow.

In the Bible, we read stories of people going through really hard things (and sometimes for a really long time). The Israelites wandered around in the desert for forty years wondering if they would ever make it to the land God promised them. Sarah and Abraham longed to have a child for years and years. Job's entire family passed away, and he was left sick and covered in sores. It all sounds so super hard, right? It was! But God will never leave His people alone in the hard moments. In fact, because of who He is (a good God), you can always have hope.

Hope is the reminder that there's a bigger plan, that the ways things are will eventually come to an end. Hope is the night light in a really dark room. Hope is that jump in your chest when you realize *something good is coming*. Hope is found in Jesus, and because He is always with us, we hold onto hope.

Rest in that.

God, thank You for always being with me when I don't feel well or when things are hard in other ways. Will You take the pain away? And while I wait, will You help me have hope every day?

DAY 98

When You Need Some Quiet

[Jesus] said to them, "Come away by yourselves to a remote place and rest for a while." For many people were coming and going, and they did not even have time to eat.—MARK 6:31

Has your house ever been so noisy that you couldn't fall asleep? Maybe your parents were chatting *and* the TV was turned up too loudly *and* your brother and his friends were in the room next door playing video games. Maybe the neighbors were shooting off fireworks *and* the dogs outside wouldn't stop barking *and* the party music was blaring. Whatever your circumstances, all the noise was too distracting for you, and you kept lying there, wide awake.

Our minds can get noisy too. Most of the time we don't realize it's happening, but all the reminders, conversations, homework lists, and news from the day play back like a movie inside our heads. All at the same time.

It can get pretty noisy in our minds!

What can you do to shut out the noise? Just as you might ask your parents to turn down the TV or use headphones to block out the barking dogs, there are ways to turn down the noise in your head as you go to sleep.

Write your thoughts in a journal before bed as a way to put them somewhere until tomorrow. Listen to calming music as you fall asleep to put your mind at ease. Recite verses you've memorized to replace the unhelpful words that are swirling around.

Noise, both around you and inside your head, is not a bad thing until it distracts you or keeps you wide awake. That kind of noise also keeps us from hearing from God. When you make space for quiet and rest, you will see and hear God more clearly.

Rest in that.

God, will You help silence all the loud noise both in my head and around me so that I can hear You more clearly?

DAY 99

When You're Afraid to Go to Sleep

He will not allow your foot to slip; your Protector will not slumber. Indeed, the Protector of Israel does not slumber or sleep. The LORD protects you; the LORD is a shelter right by your side. The sun will not strike you by day or the moon by night.—PSALM 121:3–6

Do you remember the song "He's Got the Whole World in His Hands"?

Sometimes we can sing along to a song like this, just like we do to our favorite song from a movie, but we don't pay attention to what the song means. Think about the last time you held an egg in your hand. I bet you were pretty careful with it, making sure it didn't break until you were ready for it to. What about a new baby? Think about how gentle we have to be with those cute, squishy humans! We hold them as carefully as we can, making sure they feel safe and protected.

God holds the world with love, and we are safe in His hands.

When we're scared or hurting or sad or lonely, we can turn to Him. He is Almighty God, and as Psalm 121 tells us, He is always working in the world. We don't have to stay awake to make sure everything will be okay. That's in God's hands, and He wants us to rest.

So the next time someone you love gives you a hug, think about God hugging you too. His love for you is infinitely bigger than what you can imagine, and He's holding you closely to Himself no matter what else is going on around you.

Do you know what happens so often when we're held for a while by someone we love? We fall asleep.

God is still God while you are sleeping, and you are safe in His hands.

Rest in that.

God, will You remind me that I'm safe with You? I am so thankful that I don't have to be scared of nighttime. I love You!

DAY 100

The Worry Won't Last Forever

He replied, "My presence will go with you, and I will give you rest."—EXODUS 33:14

It's 1:30 in the morning as I write today's devotion. I don't normally write this late at night, but tonight I couldn't sleep. I just kept thinking about you!

We've talked so much about all the things that worry our hearts and minds, and I wanted to tell you why it matters to me that you know you can rest. It's not because I know that your body will eventually fall asleep. It's not because I know that reading before bed can calm you down. It's because I know that you can *truly* rest when you find rest in who God is.

Learning who God is—truly understanding His character, His goodness, His protection—can change the way you live. It can change the way you think. It can change the way you rest.

The things that make us scared and make us worry *will not last*.

God sent Jesus to save us because we couldn't save ourselves. Then He restored us and made us new creations—giving us the Holy Spirit, our Helper, to live in us. Jesus will return to earth one day and hit reset on it all, restoring it to the good, perfect way He intended it to be. *The broken parts won't last.*

But God does. He lives on forever, and you get to live with Him. The greatest gift is that as soon as you began a relationship with God, your forever life with Him began. He is with you now, which means you're protected. You have a Shepherd. You're not alone. You have a good Father. God is going behind you, in front of you, and beside you. Now, and always.

Rest in that.

God, You are good! I can rest because You are with me. Amen.

JOURNALING PAGES

Have you learned any specific ways to handle worry and fear from this book? What do you want to keep doing even though your time in this book is done?

_____

_____

_____

_____

_____

_____

_____

_____

_____

_____

_____

_____

_____

What have you learned about God the past one hundred days? What have you learned about yourself? Write a prayer to God to thank Him for everything He's revealed to you.

Remember These Truths

The following is a list of all the daily Scripture passages from this devotional. On this next page, write down your favorites—the ones you want to memorize and meditate on whenever you need to calm your heart and mind.

Old Testament

Genesis 1:31
Genesis 15:1
Exodus 14:14
Exodus 33:14
Numbers 6:25
Deuteronomy
  26:18–19
Deuteronomy 31:6
Joshua 1:9
1 Samuel 17:37
1 Samuel 18:1
Psalm 6:2
Psalm 16:1
Psalm 34:4
Psalm 37:4–6
Psalm 55:16
Psalm 55:17
Psalm 55:22
Psalm 94:19
Psalm 95:7
Psalm 118:24
Psalm 119:160
Psalm 121:1–2
Psalm 121:3–6
Psalm 121:7–8

Psalm 139:1
Psalm 139:12
Psalm 139:13–14
Proverbs 3:26
Proverbs 4:25
Proverbs 14:29
Proverbs 17:22
Proverbs 18:1
Proverbs 27:5–6
Isaiah 40:31
Isaiah 41:10
Isaiah 43:2
Isaiah 46:4
Isaiah 61:3
Jeremiah 17:14
Jeremiah 23:24
Jeremiah 29:11
Lamentations
  3:22–23
Habakkuk 2:1
Habakkuk 3:19
Zephaniah 3:17

New Testament

Matthew 5:9
Matthew 6:34
Matthew 11:28–30

Matthew 18:12
Mark 4:39–41
Mark 6:31
Mark 12:30–31
John 14:1
John 14:27
John 15:15
Romans 3:23–24
Romans 5:3–4
Romans 5:8
Romans 8:6
Romans 8:15–17
Romans 8:28
Romans 12:2
Romans 12:4–5
Romans 12:12
Romans 12:21
Romans 13:14
Romans 15:7
Romans 15:13
1 Corinthians 2:9
1 Corinthians
  6:19–20
1 Corinthians 10:31
1 Corinthians 15:58
2 Corinthians 1:3–4
2 Corinthians 4:17–18

2 Corinthians 12:9
Galatians 1:10
Ephesians 1:13
Ephesians 3:12
Ephesians 4:32
Philippians 3:13–14
Philippians 4:6–7
Philippians 4:8
Philippians 4:11
Philippians 4:19
Colossians 3:9–10
Colossians 3:17
Colossians 3:23–24
1 Thessalonians 5:11
1 Thessalonians
  5:16–18
2 Thessalonians 3:16
1 Timothy 2:8
1 Timothy 4:12
Titus 1:2
Hebrews 13:6
James 1:5–6
James 1:19
James 4:8
James 5:16
1 Peter 5:6–7
1 John 5:14

Index

Use this index as a way to find a devotion written about something specific you're feeling or going through. Just look for that topic in the list to find which days have to do with that subject!

Thank You

I originally wrote a very short (ten-day) version of this book as a gift for my niece's (Shelby's) tenth birthday. When plans were made to turn it into a hundred-day book, I pulled together a group of Shelby's friends, as well as her mom (my best friend and sister-in-law, Ansley) and asked them if we could talk about the things that worry them. They graciously let me ask lots of questions, and I gave them the officially unofficial name of my Board of Directors. If I needed an opinion on writing topics along the way, I texted their moms. When I got book cover options, I asked some of them to vote. And when I sat down to write each day, I pictured they were sitting across from me.

So, to my Board of Directors: Shelby, Aubrie, Emilie, Tori, Olivia, Wren, Cassidy, Ellie, and Lucy: Thank you for allowing me to get to know you. You are very much a part of this book.

To my prayer warriors: Mom, Sherri Rivers, Rita Stewart, Erika Price, and Caroline Flake: You never let me feel alone in this work, and I knew when the words weren't flowing, you were praying for God to move. And He did. Your faithful prayers helped carry me through.

To my bestie and literary agent, Caroline Green: There's no one else I would have wanted to help me with this project. Thanks for being my sounding board, a trusted voice, and for putting up with my many, many texts. You're a gift of a friend.

To my publishing team at B&H Kids: Devin Maddox, Michelle Freeman, Anna Sargeant, Mary Wiley, and Jenaye Merida: After working together years ago, who knew we'd get to partner together to create this? You made this book better, you saw my heart behind it, and you helped me put it in more girls' hands. Forever grateful.

To my friends and the entire IF:Gathering team: The way you cheered me on, checked on writing progress, prayed, sent flowers, sat with me while I wrote, listened when I was spiraling, and believed in this book will never be lost on me. I may not have kids of my own yet, but the fact that God allowed me to use this book to be a small part of your kids' lives will always make me weep. This is for your girls: Mackenzie, Harper, Caroline, Avery, Addy, Rae, Sienna, Anna Margaret, and Adelaide.

To my family: Mom, Dad, Clay, Connie, Ellie, Adam, Ansley, Shelby, and Blake: May this book leave a legacy that is not only an extension of me, but of you. I love you!

And to my God: You met me every time I sat down to write this book and gave me words You knew I needed to hear too. Thank You, Lord. *May the words of my mouth and the meditation of my heart be acceptable to you, LORD, my rock and my Redeemer (Psalm 19:14).*